Your First Interview

3rd Edition

Your First Interview

3rd Edition

By
Ron Fry

CAREER PRESS
3 Tice Road
P.O. Box 687
Franklin Lakes, NJ 07417
1-800-CAREER-1
201-848-0310 (NJ and outside U.S.)
FAX: 201-848-1727

YOUR FIRST INTERVIEW

ISBN 1-56414-188-8, $9.99

Cover design by The Visual Group

Printed in the U.S.A. by Book-mart Press

To order this title by mail, please include price as noted above, $2.50 handling per order, and $1.00 for each book ordered. Send to: Career Press, Inc., 3 Tice Road, P.O. Box 687, Franklin Lakes, NJ 07417.

Or call toll-free 1-800-CAREER-1 (NJ and Canada: 201-848-0310) to order using VISA or MasterCard, or for further information on books from Career Press.

Library of Congress Cataloging-in-Publication Data

Fry, Ronald W.
    Your first interview / Ron Fry.
       p.   cm.
    Includes index.
    ISBN 1-56414-188-8 (pbk.)
    1. Employment interviewing.   I. Title.
HF5549.5.I6F76   1996
650.14--dc20

                                            95-44590
                                            CIP

Contents

Introduction

Welcome to the real world

Trust me, this isn't
college anymore

Most hiring managers and recruiters can spot candidates who are waiting for their first interviews.

There they sit in the reception area, those impeccably dressed collegians in standard-issue interview suits.

The nervous *thump-thump-thump* of their hearts is almost audible.

They all seem afflicted with Lady Macbeth Syndrome, constantly rubbing their palms on their thighs in hopes of drying them before they have to shake the interviewer's hand.

Will you be any different?

Not likely in today's job market. While the economy has shown signs of improvement after the gloom and doom of the early years of this decade (when I was working on the second edition of this book), college graduates still face one of the toughest job-hunting climates in this century. The "economic expansion" of the 1980s is long gone. A history of economic cycles—"boom" followed by "bust," as regular as clockwork—should be reassurance that eventually things will swing all the way back. But don't hold your breath, because it clearly won't happen any time soon.

In the last edition of this book, I reported that even the venerable IBM diminished its payroll by 40,000 jobs in 1992 alone. Old "Big Blue," is still forecasting layoffs as I update this edition. According to an article in *Kiplinger's Personal Finance Magazine,* IBM was among three huge companies planning to eliminate 10,000 jobs between them by the end of 1995. However, that same issue of *Kiplinger's* also reported that while companies like IBM expect to continue to "tighten their belts," the majority of those that do also plan to turn right back around and hire new people. Some are even *stepping up* the recruiting of new graduates like you.

In fact, from January to June 1995, the American economy created 7.5 million new jobs. While many of those will be part-time and temporary jobs, it is a sign that perhaps the hemorrhaging has stopped.

The same issue of *Kiplinger's Personal Finance Magazine* forecasted the brightest job prospects in a decade for the college class of 1995. According to a survey of employers conducted by Michigan State University, 1995 college graduates should be fielding nearly 60,000 more job offers than were made to 1994 grads. The College Placement Council, an association that also tracks hiring, says that an average starting pay will be up nearly three percent.

Before you start breaking out the champagne, let me temper this good news by saying this: You're still going to have to work harder than ever to compete against all those refugees of corporate downsizings, as a well as a supply of underemployed graduates from previous years.

According to the Collegiate Employment Research Institute of Michigan State University, six months after graduation, half of the class of 1995 graduates won't have a job in their field of education. In fact, 10 percent will still be unemployed, 20 percent will be underemployed and the remaining 20 percent will have turned tail and headed for grad school.

Clearly, even a healthier economy is no guarantee that a job is going to land in your lap. This makes interviewing skills essential.

Hey, Buster!

So, as you sit out there in the waiting room, you have plenty of good reasons to be nervous. You are faced with the task of convincing a total stranger to invest company money and time in you. Indeed, selling into a competitive market is a difficult prospect.

But that's not all. You're more likely to contend with a tougher interview than your Baby Boomer counterparts because of the rapidly increasing sophistication of those doing the hiring for America's companies. Corporations are spending more money than ever before on psychological tests, honesty tests, drug tests, assessments and computerized screening systems.

They are sending recruiters and supervisors to courses on interviewing and candidate-evaluation procedures. They are subjecting candidates to more and longer interviews.

And they are using new interviewing techniques, some of which would make thumbscrews seem like an attractive alternative.

Your First Interview

Although it would be unrealistic to expect any new hire to come with a guarantee, many employers are taking that extra step to make sure they do not even *consider* someone they will quickly wish had never darkened their doors. Simply put, employers can afford to be choosy, and they've found better ways to choose. If you have not taken a lot of time to uncover the "real you" beneath the grades and athletics and clubs, don't worry. By the time you finish today's interview process, you'll be ready to lead a self-help seminar on "Getting in Touch With Your Inner Child" or some such topic.

Help is in your hands

However, the purpose of this book is to ease your anxiety, rather than add to it.

Of course, the best way to keep anxiety from hamstringing you during the interview is through preparation. Know yourself. Know the company. And if possible, know the interviewer. *Before* you're sitting in the reception area filling out an application.

This book will help you do that. It also will help you write effective letters that will get you in the door to show your stuff. It will give you a sneak preview of exactly what to expect when you're in the interview. It will even tell you what your "interview suit" should look like.

Most importantly, this book will tell you, in detail, how to conduct yourself during every phase of the interview—how to make sure you're taking the right approach once you get to know the interviewer a bit, and what you can expect to be asked.

It will tell you how to handle illegal or embarrassing questions, how to field the job offer and how to make the most of salary discussions.

Who's in charge here?

Most of the advice in this book is pure common sense. But even the most seasoned job hunters who read it might well ask, "Now, why didn't I think of that?"

The reason is quite simple: Most job candidates think of the interview in completely the wrong way. They think of it as an interrogation. And they see themselves as suspects, not as the key prospects they really are.

This book will show you that you are, to a very large degree, *in charge of the interview*. It will convince you that you are there not only to sell the company on *you*, but to make sure that you are sold on *the company*.

Simply put, the interview is not a police lineup. It is a two-way street—an exchange of information by two or more responsible adults.

What's the worst that can happen?

As you ready yourself for any particularly stressful situation—an important exam, a big date, *your first interview*—it's helpful to put things in perspective by asking, "Well, what's the worst that can happen?"

Your First Interview

Here are some true-life stories:

- One candidate, who was extremely nervous at the start of the interview, reached across the interviewer's desk to deliver his resume and split his suit jacket wide open, explaining, "I knew Dad's clothes didn't quite fit."

- One man continually asked the director of human resources if he could phone his psychiatrist to make sure he was answering the questions correctly.

- A candidate at one company lay down on the floor through the entire interview, taking the hiring manager's advice to "relax" perhaps too literally.

If you're well-prepared—and relatively sane—it's unlikely that any of these mishaps will befall you. Preparation is the key to scoring well during the interview process. Just follow the advice in this book and you're sure to be one of the best candidates that interviewer has ever seen. So, don't worry. Read on!

Chapter 1

Developing a personal inventory

Getting to know *you*

What constantly astounds personnel people about college students going for their first job is how unprepared they are. These professionals tell me that so many inexperienced job seekers think they can just "wing it," that the majority of them usually end up tongue-tied over the most common interview questions.

For example, the most common job interview question of all time—"How would you describe yourself?"—hits most first-time job seekers like a stun gun. A typical candidate searches his or her brain frantically for the right answer to this seemingly innocuous question.

Your personal inventory

This common interview question is not at all innocuous. It can make or break the job interview. As a job candidate, you should view this question as a wonderful opportunity to sell yourself to a prospective employer. It may be the only time during the whole job-hunting process that you can talk freely, highlighting those very things that make you uniquely qualified for employment.

Unfortunately, most candidates wind up hemming and hawing and growing more and more nervous until they end up knocking a chair over on the way out. Memorable exit—no job.

Most candidates, most people in general for that matter, don't really have an answer for, "How would you describe yourself?" or more simply put, "Who are you?"

Gosh, I never thought of that

They don't know the answer because they've probably never *really* thought about the question. Most people are uncomfortable with introspection. And let's face it, the days immediately before and after graduation seem like the wrong time for contemplating your navel.

However, it is essential for you to take time out now to get to know yourself better. You might be getting through school with flying colors, but you'll flunk out of the job market unless you take time to perform a personal inventory.

Information at your fingertips

Have you put together a resume?

"Of course," you say. "Well, that process should have provided all of the information you need to answer the question, 'Who are you?' in a way that will knock the interviewer's socks off." Most candidates go about putting together a resume as if it were merely a catalog of their accomplishments and education. A resume should also be a reflection of the real you behind the facts and dates.

You must look at the process of putting together your resume as a chance to examine those qualities that make you special and those you'd like to improve. It is also an opportunity to organize a great deal of information about your education, the jobs you've held and your volunteer activities.

How you should put together a resume is discussed at length in this book. Here's a brief look at the process:

Take some time to assemble all of the following information. (Keeping separate folders with pertinent data, citations, notes, etc., is an excellent idea.)

Your employment history

Record the following details about every part-time or full-time job you've ever held. For each job, include:

- Your employer's name, address and telephone number.
- The name of your supervisor.
- The exact dates you worked.
- The approximate numbers of hours per week you worked.
- Your specific duties and responsibilities.
- Any specific skills you utilized on the job.
- Specific accomplishments and honors.
- Copies of awards and/or letters of recommendation.

Your volunteer activities

The fact that you weren't paid for a specific job—such as stuffing envelopes for a local political candidate, running a car wash to raise money for the homeless or manning a drug hotline—is no reason to leave it off your resume. Assemble the same detailed notes on each volunteer activity you've participated in, including:

- The organization's name, address and telephone number.
- The name of your supervisor.
- The exact dates you worked.
- The approximate number of hours per week you worked.
- Your specific duties and responsibilities.
- Any specific skills you utilized on the job.
- Specific accomplishments and honors.
- Copies of awards and/or letters of recommendation.

Your extracurricular activities

List all sports, clubs or other activities in which you've participated, either inside or outside of school. For each, you should include:

- The name of the activity, club or group.
- The purpose of the club/activity.
- Any office(s) you held.

- Your specific duties and responsibilities.
- Specific achievements, accomplishments and/or awards you received.

Your honors and awards

Even if some of these honors are previously listed, you should record specific data about every honor or award you've received, including:

- The name and date of the award or honor.
- Who presented it to you.
- What it was for.
- Any other pertinent details.

Your military record

If you're ever served in the military, be sure to record your complete history, including:

- The dates you served.
- The final rank you were awarded.
- Your duties and responsibilities.
- Any citations and/or awards you received.
- An explanation of specific training and/or special schooling you received.
- Specific skills you developed during your service.
- Your specific accomplishments.

At the end of this chapter, I have included eight data input sheets (with multiple copies of some, where needed). The first six cover employment, volunteer work, education, activities and awards. The last two—which cover military service and language skills—are important if, of course, they apply to you.

Here are some pointers on how to fill out these all-important data input sheets:

Employment data input sheet: Prepare one employment data input sheet for each paying job you've ever held—no matter how short the duration (yes, summer jobs count) or how limited you may think the experience was.

I've included two employment data input sheets for you to use; however, you may photocopy the worksheet as many times as necessary to include all of your job experiences.

For each job, you will need to record the basic information—employer's name, address and phone number, dates of employment and your supervisor's name—for your own files. You'll probably want to ask some of the people you've listed to provide references for you. Most prospective employers will ask you for a list of references at some point during the interviewing process.

Whether or not they provide references, these people may become great "connections"—able to provide information and referrals that will move your job search forward. Add them to your master networking list.

Describe your duties (what you did on the job) in a one- or two-sentence paragraph. For example, if you worked as a hostess in a restaurant, this section might read:

> *"Responsible for the delivery of 250 meals at dinner time and the supervision of 20 waiters and busboys. Coordinated reservations. Responsible for check and payment verification."*

Under "Skills utilized," enumerate specific capabilities that were necessary for you to perform the job, as well as any skills you developed while you had it.

If you achieved specific results (developed a new filing system, collected over $5,000 in previously assumed bad debt or instituted an award-winning art program, for example), list them. And don't be modest. Ditto, if you've ever received any award, citation or other honor (perhaps you were named Employee of the Month three times or received the company Citation for Innovation).

Volunteer work data input sheet: Treat any volunteer work, no matter how basic or short, as if it were a paying job and record the same information about it. Again, it is especially important to note specific duties and responsibilities, skills required or developed and any accomplishments or achievements you can point to as evidence of your success.

Educational data input sheets: If you're in college, omit details on high school. If you're a graduate student, list details on both graduate and undergraduate course work. If you have not yet graduated, list your anticipated date of graduation. If graduation is still more than a year away, indicate the number of credits you've already earned through the most recent semester to be completed.

Activities data input sheet: This is where to list your participation in such activities as the student government, Winter Carnival press committee or math club. Don't forget your participation on sports teams or any community or church groups. If you were elected to any offices or served on any committees in clubs, groups or on teams, by all means list each one.

Awards and honors data input sheet: List awards and honors from your school (prestigious high school awards can still be included here, even if you're in graduate school), community groups, religious groups and clubs.

Military service data input sheet: The armed forces can provide excellent training. A military stint often hastens the maturation process, making you a more attractive candidate. So if you have served in the military, you'll want to have the details ready to discuss with prospective employers during the interview.

Language data input sheet: In this global economy, employers are beginning to seek out people who are bicultural, bilingual or at least have conversational fluency in one or more language(s) other than English. One year of college French doesn't count, but if you spent a year studying abroad, you're probably fluent or near-fluent. You'll want to highlight your language proficiency and international experiences if you hope to work abroad.

While you should use these forms to summarize all of the data you have collected, do not throw away any of the specific information—report cards, transcripts, citations—just because it is recorded on these worksheets. Keep all your records in your files. After all, you never know when you might need them again!

Digging deeper

Once you fill in these forms, you'll see that they contain a great deal of information. But all they really reveal about you is what you've done and where you've been. These facts alone will not ordinarily land you a job. Now, you must take some time to think over your personal history so that you will be prepared to present the real you during the interview. Use the following questions as a guide:

1. What achievements did you take most pride in school or during your brief work experience? Why? How and why were you able to achieve these successes? What bearing will these achievements have on your career success? Why?

2. What failures in your life do you think about most often? Why did they happen? Have you done anything to keep them from occurring again? Have you learned from your mistakes? What? How?

3. How do you interact with authority figures such as bosses, teachers, parents? Do these interactions show the promise of success or failure with bosses you'll have down the line? How?

This exercise will be most effective if you write down your answers. Because it's for your eyes only, you needn't be concerned about producing beautiful prose, or, for that matter, even complete sentences. The only important thing is honesty.

Confronting yourself

If you have been completely frank, this exercise probably told you things about yourself you never realized. It may even have been difficult to confront some of your failures and examine the lessons you learned from them.

Well, don't think you're out of the woods yet. You still haven't gotten to the real you. So grab another piece of paper and write down your answers to a few searching questions:

1. What games and sports do you enjoy? What does the way you play these games say about you? Are you overly competitive? Do you give up too easily? Are you a good loser or a bad winner? Do you rise to a challenge or back away?

2. What kinds of friends do you tend to have? Do you only look for people who are very similar to you? Do you tolerate differences? Do you look for people who will laugh at all of your jokes? What are the things that have caused you to break up friendships? What does this say about you?

3. If you were to ask a group of friends and acquaintances to describe you, what adjectives would they use? List all of them. Why would people describe you in this way? Are there specific behaviors, skills, achievements or failures that lead to the use of these adjectives? What are they?

The whole picture

Now, look over all that you've written down so far and distill it into several lists with the following headings:

- My strongest skills.
- The areas in which I am most knowledgeable.
- The strongest parts of my personality.
- The things I do best.
- The skills that I should develop to do well in my career.
- The parts of my personality I could stand to improve.

If you take the time to do this exercise honestly and thoroughly, you will be amazed at the results. It should help you realize things about yourself that you never knew or, more accurately, that you never *knew* you knew.

Once more, with feeling

I urge you to engage in this process of self-examination, even if there is no imminent need to use the information. Then, when you set up your first interview, take out your lists along with another clean sheet of paper and answer the following questions:

1. What in my personal inventory will convince this employer that I deserve the position for which I am going to interview?

2. What are the strengths, achievements, skills and areas of knowledge that make me most qualified for this position? What in my background should separate me from the pack of candidates for the position?

3. What weaknesses should I admit to, if asked about them, and how will I indicate that I have improved or will improve them?

A little knowledge is a dangerous thing

The failure to perform a personal inventory means that you will not be fully prepared for your interview. Knowing yourself a little better, on the other hand, will help build your self-confidence. You'll know that you are going into the interview prepared to answer the toughest questions any inquisitor can throw at you.

I hope that this first chapter has convinced you of the importance of doing your homework before the interview. If not, the next few chapters will demonstrate just how essential that homework will be.

EMPLOYMENT DATA INPUT SHEET

Employer Name: _____

Address: _____

Address: _____

Phone: _____

Dates of Employment: _____ to _____

Hours Per Week: _____ Salary/Pay: _____

Supervisor's Name & Title: _____

Duties: _____

_____

_____

Skills Utilized: _____

_____

_____

Accomplishments/Honors/Awards: _____

_____

_____

Other Important Information: _____

_____

Your First Interview

EMPLOYMENT DATA INPUT SHEET

Employer Name: _____

Address: _____

Address: _____

Phone: _____

Dates of Employment: _____ to _____

Hours Per Week: _____ Salary/Pay: _____

Supervisor's Name & Title: _____

Duties: _____

_____

_____

Skills Utilized: _____

_____

_____

Accomplishments/Honors/Awards: _____

_____

_____

Other Important Information: _____

_____

VOLUNTEER WORK DATA INPUT SHEET

Organization Name: _____

Address: _____

Address: _____

Phone: _____ Hours Per Week: _____

Dates of Activity: _____

Supervisor's Name & Title: _____

Duties: _____

_____

_____

Skills Utilized: _____

_____

_____

Accomplishments/Honors/Awards: _____

_____

_____

Other Important Information: _____

_____

_____

_____

VOLUNTEER WORK DATA INPUT SHEET

Organization Name: _____

Address: _____

Address: _____

Phone: _____ Hours Per Week: _____

Dates of Activity: _____

Supervisor's Name & Title: _____

Duties: _____

_____

_____

Skills Utilized: _____

_____

_____

Accomplishments/Honors/Awards: _____

_____

_____

Other Important Information: _____

_____

_____

_____

HIGH SCHOOL DATA INPUT SHEET

School Name: _____

Address: _____

Phone: _____ Years Attended: _____

Major Studies: _____

GPA/Class Rank: _____

Honors: _____

Important Courses: _____

_____

OTHER SCHOOL DATA INPUT SHEET

School Name: _____

Address: _____

Phone: _____ Years Attended: _____

Major Studies: _____

GPA/Class Rank: _____

Honors: _____

Important Courses: _____

_____

COLLEGE DATA INPUT SHEET

College: _____

Address: _____

Phone: _____ Years Attended: _____

Degrees Earned: _____ Major: _____

Minor: _____ Honors: _____

_____

Important Courses: _____

_____

GRADUATE SCHOOL DATA INPUT SHEET

College: _____

Address: _____

Phone: _____ Years Attended: _____

Degrees Earned: _____ Major: _____

Minor: _____ Honors: _____

_____

Important Courses: _____

_____

ACTIVITIES DATA INPUT SHEET

Club/Activity: _____

Office(s) Held: _____

Description of Participation: _____

_____

Duties/Responsibilities: _____

_____

Club/Activity: _____

Office(s) Held: _____

Description of Participation: _____

_____

Duties/Responsibilities: _____

_____

Club/Activity: _____

Office(s) Held: _____

Description of Participation: _____

_____

Duties/Responsibilities: _____

_____

ACTIVITIES DATA INPUT SHEET

Club/Activity: _____

Office(s) Held: _____

Description of Participation: _____

_____

Duties/Responsibilities: _____

_____

Club/Activity: _____

Office(s) Held: _____

Description of Participation: _____

_____

Duties/Responsibilities: _____

_____

Club/Activity: _____

Office(s) Held: _____

Description of Participation: _____

_____

Duties/Responsibilities: _____

_____

AWARDS & HONORS DATA INPUT SHEET

Name of Award, Citation, Etc.: _____

From Whom Received: _____

Date: _____ Significance: _____

_____

Other Pertinent Information: _____

_____

Name of Award, Citation, Etc.: _____

From Whom Received: _____

Date: _____ Significance: _____

_____

Other Pertinent Information: _____

_____

Name of Award, Citation, Etc.: _____

From Whom Received: _____

Date: _____ Significance: _____

_____

Other Pertinent Information: _____

_____

MILITARY SERVICE DATA INPUT SHEET

Branch: _____

Rank (at Discharge): _____

Dates of Service: _____

Duties & Responsibilities: _____

_____

_____

_____

Special Training and/or School Attended: _____

_____

_____

_____

Citations, Awards, etc.: _____

_____

_____

Specific Accomplishments: _____

_____

_____

_____

LANGUAGE DATA INPUT SHEET

Language: _____

    ❑ Read   ❑ Write   ❑ Converse

Background (number of years studied, travel, etc.): _____

_____

_____

_____

Language: _____

    ❑ Read   ❑ Write   ❑ Converse

Background (number of years studied, travel, etc.): _____

_____

_____

_____

Language: _____

    ❑ Read   ❑ Write   ❑ Converse

Background (number of years studied, travel, etc.): _____

_____

_____

_____

Chapter 2

The importance of company research

Getting to know *them*

For most people, preparing for a first job interview is an exercise in self-absorption.

They spend days polishing their resumes and devote hours to selecting the right outfits and making sure every strand of hair is in place. They practice, practice, practice—to be sure they'll be ready to talk for hours about themselves and the traits that will make them terrific employees.

What's wrong with being prepared, you ask? Not a thing. But if all focus on is you before showing up for your first interview, you will still arrive *un*prepared. You will have left out perhaps the most important step of all.

The best preparation for any job interview involves looking beyond the mirror. You must take the time to learn about the company for which you hope to work, the job for which you are interviewing and, if possible, the interviewer you will be meeting.

This is important not only as a means of enhancing your performance during the job interview, but also as an assurance that your first career move is the right one for you. How do you know that you want to work for a company until you've adequately researched it? Failure to research a company adequately might mean that within weeks (or less) of sliding behind your new desk, you'll wonder why you ever agreed to work there in the first place!

Getting critical information about prospective employers is often not particularly difficult, although it might well be time-consuming. But such detailed company research is probably the key step most first-time interviewers skip.

What kind of salesperson are you?

To understand the importance of pre-interview preparation, think of yourself as a salesperson. Would you call on a potential customer without knowing anything about his or her business? If you did, how would you go about convincing that person that he or she needs your product? Would selling thousands of dollars of your product without knowing how well he or she was doing—whether the business was even financially sound—make sense?

Of course not. Then why do so many candidates show up for job interviews with only the vaguest knowledge about the company, even though they are there to sell their most important product—themselves?

Virtually every interviewer will ask a candidate what questions he or she has about the company. This is not merely the interviewer's way of being polite. It is a very effective technique to gauge *your* interest in the company— an important component of whether *the company* should be interested in you.

Starting your detective work

The best place to start your investigation is your college placement office or library. Look for these reference tools:

- *The Career Advisor Series* (Gale Research Inc.).

- *College Placement Directory* (Zimmerman & Lavine).

- *College Placement Annual* (College Placement Council).

- Dun & Bradstreet's various directories.

- *F&S Index of Corporations and Industries.*

- Fitch Corporations Manuals.

- Moody's Manuals.

- *MacRae's Bluebook.*

- *Standard & Poor's Register of Corporations, Directors and Executives.*

- *Thomas Register of American Companies.*

While all of these resources can be invaluable, the one I recommend most highly is the *F&S Index*. It lists published articles by industry and company. This will help you obtain objective information about the latest developments at a company and in an industry. It can help you find many articles that will arm you with terrific, up-to-date knowledge about the company you're interviewing with. And this is just the right kind of information that will help you impress an interviewer.

However, because many of the new jobs are being created by very small companies, or microenterprises, you may not find much in the standard reference resources listed above. If your initial research proves fruitless or only marginally productive, try the following outside sources of information:

- The **chamber of commerce** in the community that's home to the company or division. You can find out how the company has been performing. Has it been growing or shrinking? How many people does it employ? How many did it employ in the community two years ago? Do people consider it a good place to work?

- **Business/industry associations.** Consult the *Encyclopedia of Associations* (Gale Research) to find out the names of trade and professional organizations to which the company might belong. Ask a research or public relations representative the same questions you asked the chamber of commerce.

- **Executive, professional and technical placement agencies.** If you are getting the job interview through an agent, see how much you can learn about the prospective employer from him or her.

- **Business editors.** Turn the tables on the news media: Ask *them* the questions! A community newspaper's business reporter or editor will usually be the person most knowledgeable about local companies. They'll know about developments at particular companies, how employees like working for them and how they are viewed by the community.

- **Trade magazines.** Every industry has at least one trade magazine covering its developments. Call a junior (assistant or associate) editor on the staff who, most likely, is not much older than you. Ask if the publication has covered the company and if you can receive copies of the article(s).

- **School alumni.** The college placement office, your fraternity/sorority or alumni association might be able to tell you about someone working at the company. Alumni are usually happy to help someone from their alma mater who's about to enter the job market, so pick up the phone.

- **Stockbrokers/analysts.** If the company is public, it will have an investor relations representative who can tell you which brokers and analysts "follow the stock." This means that a representative of the brokerage has visited with the company, written a detailed report for investors and analyzed its industry, balance sheet and management. Call the brokerage and ask for a copy of the report. It will be objective, very revealing and it'll give you terrific material with which you can impress the interviewer.

- **Books.** There were a number of business books that hit the market during the 1980s that can help you get a better understanding of a company or industry. Your library will have some of the titles dealing with well-known corporations. To find others, again, I recommend calling the trade associations.

- **Online services.** With a computer, modem and the appropriate software, you can tap into the vast resources of the Internet or navigate within the more manageable environs of commercial services, such as CompuServe and America Online. (Even if you don't have the right equipment, many libraries can help you launch online "expeditions.") There are currently a multitude of bulletin boards, databases and discussion groups through which you can track down sometimes obscure information to impress a prospective employer in an interview. For example, you might be able to garner some "inside" information about a specific industry or employer by chatting with someone in an online discussion group. Just be sure to keep an eye on the clock! Spending an hour or so a day browsing databases and chatting with others on the Internet or a commercial service can cost you from $20 to $40 per month. Those online minutes add up.

Profiting from inside information

Once you've culled the *outside*—and probably more objective—sources of information, take a look at what the company tells the public about itself. After you have the interview lined up, call the interviewer's secretary or the company's investor relations department to obtain the following:

- **Annual reports.** Mark Twain said that there are three kinds of lies—"lies, damned lies and statistics"—and you'll find all of them in most annual reports. Read between the lines (and the lies) of the annual report to learn as much as you can about the company.

  You will be able to tell how the company's sales and profits have been increasing or decreasing over the past few years, what the company's plans are for the year ahead and the health of the industry in which the company operates.

  In addition, an annual report should indicate how the company feels about its employees. Note whether the company talks about accomplishments of particular employees. Does it have photos of people at work? Or does it stick strictly to "the numbers" and vague musings of the chairman?

- **Employee handbooks.** Be gutsy. Ask the company to send you a copy of this valuable document. At the very least, the handbook will tell you about benefits, vacation time, salary review policies and other information you might not want to ask about in the interview. It also should give you valuable insights into the company's attitude toward its employees. Is in-house training provided? Is the company picnic a much-anticipated annual event?

- **Sales/marketing brochures.** Knowing about a company's products will help you determine whether you'd like to work for the organization and give you material upon which to base questions.

Homework can pay off

I know of one candidate, a marketing major, who spent a great deal of time poring over the brochures from an aerospace contractor. During his initial interview, he stunned the recruiter by knowing so much about the company's guidance systems. In fact, the candidate relieved the interviewer of the task he hated to perform most—explaining the company's complicated technology!

What to ask campus recruiters

Although on-campus recruiting is becoming increasingly rare these days, you may be one of the lucky ones. What do you do if your first contact with a company is through a recruiter who has come to harvest the best and brightest students from your graduating class?

When you meet with a recruiter, don't be content to sit there and answer his or her questions. Make it your goal to find out information that will help *you* ease on down the interview road.

Ask about the company's products. What other students from your school has the company hired in the past? How have they fared? Who will make the final hiring decision for the position in which you're interested?

Ask the recruiters, if they seem interested in you, to send you the annual reports, product brochures and other materials mentioned previously.

The answers to your questions

Now that you know where to find information about prospective employers, here are specific questions for which you should be seeking equally specific answers:

- What are the company's leading products? What products is it looking to introduce in the near future?

- What are the company's key markets? How strong are these markets? What is the company's share of these markets?

- What are the prospects for growth and expansion? Does the company plan to grow internally or through mergers and acquisitions?

- What rate of growth does the company project over the next few years?

- To what does the company attribute fluctuations in sales?

- Has the company "downsized" or reorganized recently? What were the extent of layoffs and early retirements?

- Do reductions of staff seem likely in the near future?

Finding out about the interviewer

Now comes the toughest detective work of all—finding out a little bit about the person who will be firing the questions at you. This is not very important for your meeting with the recruiter in the human resources department, but it is crucial for your meeting with the hiring manager.

Let's face it, in the initial interview, you'll have perhaps 45 minutes to convince someone that you're the best candidate for the job. It probably will help to know which are the right buttons to push to get the interviewer to notice—and *remember*—you.

Tim, a business associate of mine, asked the personnel department to send him as many back issues as it could of the company newsletter when he was preparing to be interviewed for an open position. He then devoured the newsletters, studying everything from the opening letter from the president of the company to the birth and wedding announcements. This enabled him to begin questions like this: "I've read that your company has recently installed a computer-integrated manufacturing system...."

Tim also learned that the company had been increasing its sales volume substantially, which led him to ask some informed questions about the company's successes. He told me that he could sense how impressed the interviewer was that he had done so much research on the company.

But that was just the start of Tim's use of his research. The newsletters told him that his interviewer, Mr. Marty, had been with the company for 20 years and worked his way up from a lower-level job in the distribution department.

The biography in the newsletter also indicated that Marty was an avid bird-watcher. Tim did a bit of research into bird-watching—just enough to make some intelligent comments about the pictures on Marty's walls—and framed questions that demonstrated a willingness to follow a career path similar to the one his prospective boss had.

One of your key goals of the interview is to stand out in bold relief from the other candidates for the position. Tim's efforts clearly helped him do just that.

Showing your stuff without showing off

The old saying, "If you've got it, flaunt it," is, in some ways, bad advice when it comes to interviewing for a job.

While you'll definitely want to demonstrate that you've prepared for this interview, have researched the company thoroughly and prepared a list of informed questions, avoid overdoing it.

Flaunting your research will have two very negative consequences:

1. You will sound like a stock analyst's report that has been wired for sound.

2. You will probably show up the interviewer somewhere along the line. Odds are, the interviewer didn't read the annual report the night before your appointment, so he or she won't be as familiar with its details as you are. *Don't embarrass the interviewer!*

The best thing to do—and you'll read this throughout the book—is to relax and be yourself. If you have, indeed, done a lot of research on the company, that fact will become apparent by the questions you ask and the answers you give.

Work your research into your conversation with the interviewer deftly and as unobtrusively as possible. Don't hit him or her over the head with the encyclopedia of ABC Widget.

Two other important points to remember:

1. You cannot learn anything if you are doing all the talking—or thinking of how you're going to impress the interviewer next. You don't just want to sell yourself to the company during your job interview. You want to give the company every opportunity to sell itself to *you*. The more of the interviewer's time you take up showing off your knowledge, the less he or she will learn about the real you. And the less you'll learn from the interviewer.

2. People are more likely to hire, or recommend for hire, people they like. Not too many people like show-offs who enjoy hearing themselves talk.

Learn more during the interview

Solid research also will prepare you to learn everything you want about the company before the conclusion of the interview. It will help you frame questions that will turn the interview into a two-way street, a learning experience for you as well as your "inquisitors."

If you've read that the organization is family-owned, find out how this might affect your prospects for promotion. If the newsletter reported that an employee opinion poll had been taken, discreetly ask for some of the results.

Asking about some of these areas can be rather delicate. We'll talk about how to frame your questions (so they are taken as brilliant indications of your interest and not insulting examples of your insensitivity!) in Chapter 10.

Another important tool for doing research on prospective employers is the informational interview, which we will discuss fully in Chapter 4.

Chapter 3

Landing the interview

Homework really does pay off

Although nobody likes doing it, homework does have its payoffs. Especially during a job hunt. From the research you doggedly pursued on each prospective employer, you should have learned several important things:

- What the company is looking for in its employees.

- What the company's key products and markets are.

- Whether the company has hired employees from your school, with your degree, and how they've fared.

- Who the hiring manager is and what type of people he or she usually hires.

- Why you might enjoy working for the organization.

All of this information will prove invaluable to you, not only during the interview, but in helping you get the interview in the first place.

Who can you turn to?

Whether you're answering a classified advertisement or launching an all-out direct-mail assault on the best companies in the industry you've chosen, you'll want to write to the hiring manager, *not* the human resources department.

The reason is quite simple: Human resources departments usually have little idea about what the hiring manager really wants in a job applicant. The more technical or specialized the field, the truer this statement.

I've known of a human resources director who recommended a candidate for whom English was a second—and not very *good*—language for the top editorial post on a major association magazine. Another passed along a candidate who got 55 out of 100 on a spelling test for a proofreading position. Still another recommended someone whose resume was filled with rather obvious or easily discovered lies for a vice president of finance position.

At many organizations, hiring managers make it a point to go around the human resources department—bringing candidates in, interviewing them and only *then* passing them along so human resources can take care of the paperwork.

Make it easier for the hiring manager to do just that. Make every effort to get in touch with him or her yourself.

That winning letter

The letter on page 56 was written by a candidate who is about to get out of college and stride tentatively into the workaday world. Let's take a look at several of the key components of this letter:

1. It's typed on the applicant's letterhead. A professional touch. Design and print your own letterhead and envelopes. Use a quality letter stock in white, off-white or buff. (Your resume should be printed on the same stock.)

   Also note that the typeface used is not too fancy. It is a common, readable style.

2. It addresses, by name and title, the manager with the authority to hire him. (Naturally the applicant had the good sense and professionalism to triple-check the spelling of both the name and title! Even simple first and last names, like Steven/Stephen or Green/Greene can trip you up.)

3. The first paragraph immediately states the reason the applicant wrote the letter. It indicates the specific job or type of work for which he was applying and where (or from whom) he learned about the opening.

4. The second and third paragraphs contain his sales pitch. Tell the hiring manager why he or she should consider you for the job, what you offer the company and why you deserve an interview.

5. It's lively. It refers to the resume and tells the hiring manager a little more about the candidate without overdoing it.

Let's face it, as a college student, you don't have too much experience to sell to a prospective employer. It's important to mention such things as internships, but don't oversell them.

6. It mentions the name of the company and some fact about it. This sets the letter apart from so many of the form letters job seekers send out.

7. This letter provides absolutely no information that is not related to the job. If a manager wants to learn more, he or she will make an attempt do so during the interview. But he or she is probably not interested in slogging through a lot of extraneous information in a letter.

8. It's important to keep the letter to one page, as did this candidate. Anything more might lead some managers to toss it.

A couple of other cautions: Always type, never handwrite, the manager's name and address on the envelope, no matter how inconvenient your word processor or typewriter makes this process. And, if you have a summer job, do not send the letter through your employer's postage meter. It makes you look like a petty crook. Spring for your own stamp.

You've got it covered

Why is the cover letter so important? Well, we've established that it is best for you to apply for your job with the hiring manager. A letter addressed to that person will be read, particularly if you mark the envelope "personal and confidential."

Even if the manager asked his or her assistant to screen all of his mail, a letter marked "personal" will probably not be opened. The assistant is more likely to pass your letter and resume on to the manager, rather than the human resources department.

Okay, sometimes you should use human resources

I have stressed the importance of writing your letter to the real decision-maker, the hiring manager. However, it sometimes *is* advisable to contact the human resources department, especially given your current lack of experience.

If you have targeted a particular company, but are not sure whether any job openings exist, get in touch with the director of human resources, again, by name. Tell him or her the reasons that you'd like to work for the company, the positions you think you'd be qualified for and something about yourself and your accomplishments.

A former colleague of mine, Charlie, wanted to work in the public relations department of one of the large pharmaceutical houses in New Jersey. His reasons: The company had consistently been cited in business magazines and textbooks as one of the best-run in America, and it spent more money on developing new products than any other company in the industry.

Gregory L. Wright
104 Highland Avenue
Yorktown Heights, NY 11345
914-555-1237

February 24, 1996

Mr. Robert Carr, Vice President, Sales
ABC Sportswear
1315 Broadway
New York, NY 10036

Dear Mr. Carr:

The sales trainee position at ABC Sportswear briefly described in your February 23 advertisement in *The New York Times* is very appealing to me. Please accept this letter and the attached resume as application for this opening.

While majoring in business (with a marketing minor) at Wallace State, I worked on a number of special projects that helped me develop some of the skills mentioned in your ad. Specifically, I gained a great deal of knowledge about budgeting, telemarketing and account analysis.

As a summer intern for Reebok, I was able to refine some of my skills as I worked with the promotion department to develop a sales-call management system. My internship at Shaw Electronics gave me experience in helping establish a database marketing program.

I would like to meet with you at your convenience to discuss this position and my qualifications for it in more detail. I learned a great deal about ABC from your campus recruiter, Nick Deane, and think it would be a terrific place to work.

Thank you for your time. I look forward to meeting with you.

Sincerely yours,

Gregory Wright

Gregory Wright

Charlie networked like crazy. He asked everyone he knew if they knew anyone at the company. Finally, he came across someone whose friend's father, a Mr. Jones, worked there. He got in touch with the friend and asked if he could call his dad. Mr. Jones was delighted to be contacted. Charlie asked Mr. Jones if he knew the head of the public relations department and whether he knew of any openings.

The man did, in fact, know the head of P.R., but wasn't sure about openings. My friend asked if he could use Mr. Jones's name in a letter, and Mr. Jones, after spending some time with Charlie, graciously said yes.

Charlie practically ran to his typewriter and composed the letter on page 59.

The follow-up phone call

You've sealed your message in the bottle and thrown it out to sea. The optimists among you will expect your telephones to ring off the hook with job offers within two days. Pessimists will expect to hear nothing.

Unfortunately, in most cases, the pessimists are right. When your letter produces nothing, you probably will feel depressed. You just won't believe that some lucky company out there has been given the chance to hire you and hasn't jumped at it. It's probably unrealistic of you to feel quite so surprised. After all, that company you're interested in working for *has* been thriving without you for some time.

What do you do? Well, to borrow a phrase from sales-motivation speakers, "Make it happen!" And the way to make it happen, as every salesperson knows, is to follow up your letter with a phone call.

Your First Interview

I suggest waiting about a week after you've posted your letter to call. However, I advise against calling on Monday or Friday, first thing in the morning, toward 5 p.m. or during the lunch shift. In other words, place your call between 10 a.m. and noon or between 2:30 p.m. and 4 p.m. on Tuesday, Wednesday or Thursday.

Odds are you won't get through to the Bastings and Carrs of the world. You'll get secretaries, receptionists, message desks and, increasingly these days, voice-mail or answering machines. Here's the way a typical conversation might proceed:

Secretary: *Mr. Basting's office.*

You: *Hello, I'm wondering if Mr. Basting is available. My name is Charles Goett.*

S: *What is this about, Mr. Goett?*

Y: *I sent a letter to Mr. Basting on July 1. Do you know if he's received it?*

S: *What was it regarding?*

Y: *I was writing to inquire about possible openings in your department.*

S: *Well, I don't know of any openings at this time. But I'll see that Mr. Basting gets your message.*

Y: *When do you expect that I'll hear from him?*

S: *Well, he's been very busy, so I can't answer that. But I will see to it that he does get your message.*

Y: *I appreciate that. Have a nice day.*

Charles Goett
7 Lobell Court, West Orange, NJ 07009   201-748-2098

July 1, 1995

Mr. David Basting, Dir. of Public Relations
Wonder Drug, Inc.
One Wonder Plaza
Harmon Meadow, NJ 07123

Dear Mr. Basting:

I am writing at the suggestion of your colleague, Robert Jones, to inquire about possible openings in the Public Relations department at Wonder Drug, Inc. Mr. Jones mentioned that your company does hire entry-level people in your department.

Mr. Basting, it has been my dream to work in the public relations department of a prestigious company such as yours. More specifically, for the past few months I've developed a keen desire to work for Wonder Drug.

Everything I've read about your company in business magazines and leading management books convinces me that yours is one of the most well-run, innovative and decent companies in the world.

And I'm the right person for any openings you might have now or in the near future. While taking a double major in business and journalism at City State, I worked in the school's publicity office. During my summers, I interned for Engulf & Devour Public Relations, writing and trying to secure placements for releases on companies such as Bon Vivant and Alia Industries.

I would like to meet with you to discuss possible openings and my qualifications in more detail. I will call you in a week to see if we can set up an appointment.

Thank you for your time. I look forward to meeting with you.

Sincerely yours,

Charles Goett

Charles Goett

Despite the fact that you're being stonewalled, maintain a pleasant tone during such conversations. In fact, it helps if you smile while you're speaking on the phone. Smiling actually improves the tone of your delivery.

If you've cited a network connection in your letter to Mr. Basting or if your skills are a match, you'll probably hear back from him. If you don't hear back within a week or so, or by the time the secretary told you that he might call, call again. Remember, *always* be pleasant on the phone. A secretary or assistant who takes a dislike to you can be lethal to your hopes of landing a job.

"Don't call us..."

If your second phone call produces nothing, you'll know that you're in a "don't-call-us-we'll-call-you" situation. It's probably best to give up unless you have another connection that you can follow up.

If you receive a letter acknowledging receipt of your resume, but rejecting your application, follow up with a note thanking the person for responding and asking him or her to keep you in mind for any future openings.

The letter should read something like the one on page 62—it shows that you are attentive, courteous and somewhat aggressive. It also helps ensure that the only reason you didn't hear from Basting is because your letter scored a quick two points in his secretary's "circular file."

What if they *do* call you

If, on the other hand, someone calls you with a positive response to your letter, stay calm—and don't drop the phone!

In fact, you should be at least somewhat prepared for this to happen. An increasing number of companies are pre-screening candidates on the telephone to save time and reduce recruitment costs.

The hiring manager or a representative from the human resources department will have a battery of questions for you. We will discuss the content of these questions in Chapter 5. Relax. You'll be ready.

If you do secure the interview, follow up with a confirming note. It should read like the letter on page 63.

Well, the easy part is over. You've secured your chance to interview for a job. You've done your homework on the company. You've written the best letter of your life. And you've sold yourself in writing and over the telephone.

But that's only the beginning. Now you must prepare and rehearse for your interview and endure the emotional seesaw between hope and dread. However, the following chapters can help assure that that emotional seesaw ends up being a joy ride.

Charles Goett
7 Lobell Court, West Orange, NJ 07009   201-748-2098

July 10, 1995

Mr. David Basting
Director of Public Relations
Wonder Drug, Inc.
One Wonder Plaza
Harmon Meadow, NJ 07123

Dear Mr. Basting:

Naturally, I was disappointed that there are no positions open for me at this time at Wonder Drug, Inc. As I indicated in my letter of July 1, I have long been an admirer of your company and thought that my skills in marketing would make me a valuable contributor.

I am enclosing another copy of my resume that I hope you will keep on file in the event that a position opens for which you think I am qualified.

I look forward to hearing from you some time in the future.

Sincerely yours,

Charles Goett

Charles Goett

Charles Goett
7 Lobell Court, West Orange, NJ 07009   201-748-2098

July 10, 1995

Mr. David Basting
Director of Public Relations
Wonder Drug, Inc.
One Wonder Plaza
Harmon Meadow, NJ 07123

Dear Mr. Basting:

I am looking forward to meeting with you on August 15 at
9:30 a.m. to discuss the opening in your department. I am very
excited about the chance to work for your company as assistant
director of solid waste management.

Thank you for the opportunity.

Sincerely yours,

Charles Goett

Charles Goett

Chapter 4

Wiring your network

Making valuable contacts and conducting effective informational interviews

Career experts estimate that as many as 80 percent of all available jobs are *never advertised!* That can put you at a real disadvantage in the current highly competitive job market. If you don't have access to the opportunities, you surely won't get the interviews.

So how can you better your position? By building on a resource you already have close at hand—your network. You don't have a network, you say? Trust me. *Everyone* has a network—family, friends, professors, past and present co-workers (you get the picture). These people also know a lot of other people (through *their* networks). In fact, they may know someone who holds the job you're interested in or, better yet, who works in the company you're targeting.

Would your uncle mind if you called or wrote a letter to his golf buddy who just happens to be a marketing manager at XYZ Company? Chances are he'll pave the way with a phone call himself. All of a sudden you have an "in."

That is how most people get jobs—through informal, personal connections.

The means *is* the end

At the outset of your career, it's tempting to think of networking as means to an end—getting your first job. But I encourage you to look farther ahead. You don't need me to remind you that these are turbulent times. Thinking realistically, chances are that you will "downsized" out of your first job in a year or so. What will you do then?

If you've kept in touch with all of the new people you added to your network this time around, your task will be that much easier next time. Yes, that means building and maintaining a mutually beneficial relationship with each of your connections.

Sounds exhausting, doesn't it? But it doesn't have to be. Rather than getting together every week, you may check in by phone once or twice a year or send off a note with an article that might be of interest to a former colleague or refer someone who, earlier, made an introduction for you.

The fact is, you can never know what twists and turns your career will take or what kind of information you'll need down the road. Your fate often lies in the quality and extent of your connections.

A web of relationships

While the term networking didn't gain prominence until the 1970s, it is by no means a new phenomenon. Attend any Ivy League school and you're automatically part of its very special centuries-old network.

Networking is the process of turning to relatives, friends and acquaintances to secure the information—and possibly even referrals!—that will help you find a job. Networking will help you identify where jobs are and give you the background and personal introductions necessary to pursue them.

Major law firms are known to favor candidates from a preferred list of law schools—typically, the same ones the senior partners attended. Washington, D.C. and corporate America have their own networks. And very often networks overlap allowing corporate bigwigs to move back and forth from the boardroom to the Cabinet Room.

Creating the ideal network

The following tips will help you identify and enrich your current network:

1. Diversify. Unlike the Harvard or Princeton networks—confined to former graduates of those particular schools—your network should be as diversified and wide-ranging as possible. You never know who might be in a position to help, so don't limit your contacts to just relatives and close friends. The more you reach out to diverse people, the greater the variety of information you will receive.

2. Include everybody. Your initial networking list should include just about every living, breathing person you know. That includes your friends, relatives, social acquaintances, classmates, college alumni, professors, teachers, dentist, doctor, family lawyer, insurance agent, banker, travel agent, elected officials in your community, clergy, members of your religious group, local tradespeople, local business owners and social club officers. Ultimately, you'll include everybody *they* know!

3. Make specific requests. Calling everyone and simply asking for "whatever help you can give me" is unfair to the people you're calling—and not very effective. Instead, make a list of the kinds of assistance you'll need from the people in your network. Then make specific requests of each person. Do they know of jobs at their company? Can they introduce you to the proper executives? Have they heard something about or know someone at the company you're planning to interview with next week? The more organized you are, the easier it will be to figure out who might have the information you need.

4. Keep in touch. Keep those who have provided helpful information or introductions informed about how it all turns out. Such courtesy will be appreciated and may lead to more contacts. If someone you call has nothing to offer today, make a note to yourself to call back in a few months. If you've taken my advice about record keeping to heart, you'll soon be able to track the dividends.

Interviewing for information

This interview works best when there is no pressure on the interviewer (your new contact) to give you a job. In an informational interview, information is the only thing you're after—information that you hope will someday get you a job, but that's *someday*.

Right now, you are the interviewer. Your goal is to learn as much as you can about the industry, company and job you've targeted. A meeting with someone already doing what you soon hope to be doing is by far the best way to find out everything you need to know before you walk through the door and sit down for a formal job interview. Don't be shy about this. You'll find that most people are happy to talk about their jobs.

If you learn of a specific job opening during an informational interview, you are in a position to find out many important details about it. You may also find out who will be doing the interviewing and, if you're lucky, gain some valuable insight into his or her experience and personality. With your contact's permission, you may also be able to use his or her name as a referral.

"But who has time to meet with me?"

As the head of a publishing company, I get several requests for such informational interviews every year. I always agree to see candidates who send well-written letters and indicate that they clearly understand that my company has no job openings.

I have several reasons for making time in a very busy schedule for such job seekers:

- My company keeps a file of promising candidates that we use when we want to add staff.

- I have colleagues and recruiters in my network to whom I want to refer good candidates.

- I like to know how my company is perceived by job seekers for competitive and recruitment concerns.

- I want to help out people in the same straits as I was in when I graduated from college.

Your First Interview

I am happy to provide an overview of the publishing market, information on starting salaries for the types of jobs these individuals are seeking, and, if I am impressed by them, to refer them to colleagues.

Candidates leave such interviews armed with valuable information that will come in handy in future interviews and, if the interview went well, with more confidence.

Setting up an informational interview

Where do you begin? Preferably in a quiet room with a piece of paper on which you will write:

1. The names of everyone you know who might be filling a job in which you're interested.

2. The names of people who might *know someone* interested in making such a hire.

If you think these lists will be short, think again, particularly about list number two. Consider:

- Your professors.
- Your parents' friends.
- Your parents' banker.
- Your family doctor.
- Your family attorney.
- Your parents' bosses.
- People who belong to your house of worship.
- The principal of your high school.
- The head of your volunteer organization.

Then, begin calling or visiting each of these people. If they don't know someone well, introduce yourself by making a *specific request*. Tell your network connection what you've studied in school, the type of job you're interested in landing and the companies you'd like to join. Ask if he or she knows someone already working in your chosen career. If, for example, your professor gives you the names and telephone numbers of some of his former students, be sure to ask if you can use his name when you call or write to these people.

I know that you might have to overcome some shyness and embarrassment to call people and ask for help. But you'll be surprised at how delighted people are that *you thought they could help you.*

The next step

In Chapter 3, I showed you how Charles Goett successfully networked his way into a job interview by contacting the father of a friend of one of his contacts, Mr. Jones. It turned out Mr. Jones was delighted to meet with Charlie and, afterward, have Charlie use his name when contacting the head of the public relations department in his company. (See how a good network resembles a web?)

Well, you'll use similar techniques to secure informational interviews.

Begin by writing letters to the people referred by your networking connections. Your letters should read something like this:

Ann Marie Sharp
1333 Stanton Avenue
Lubbock, TX 45678

April 30, 1996

Ms. Candice Burns
Vice President of Marketing
The Crimson Hotel Group
3333 LBJ Parkway
Houston, TX 46810

Dear Ms. Burns:

I am writing at the suggestion of Dan Hyman at ABC Travel. He knows of my interest in the hotel field and, given your experience at The Crimson Hotel Group, thought you might be able to help me learn more about the industry and how I might get my career off to a flying start.

As I finish up my studies at the Howard Johnson Hotel and Restaurant School at Orange County State, I am doing everything I can to gain a better understanding of the "real world" of hotel sales and marketing, my particular field of study.

If you could spare a few minutes to meet with me during the week of May 13, when I will be visiting the Houston area, I'm certain you could give me the direction I need.

I will call your office next week to see if we can schedule an appointment. I look forward to meeting you.

Sincerely,

Ann Marie Sharp

Ann Marie Sharp

cc: Dan Hyman

Notice that Ann Marie made it clear to Ms. Burns that she was well aware that Crimson might not be hiring at the time. In addition, Ann Marie sent a copy of the letter to her contact Dan Hyman so that he would remember giving the reference should Candice Burns call him.

The follow-through

Your follow-up phone calls requesting informational interviews will be similar to those Charles Goett followed in the last chapter. You'll probably be stonewalled by an executive secretary, but you should be polite and persistent.

Remember to refer to the date and subject of the letter and say, "I wrote to [Mr. or Ms. X] at the suggestion of..." This will help increase the chances that your message will go to the top of the pile.

If you are successful in landing an informational interview, send a confirming letter restating the date, time and reason for the appointment.

The informational interview

When the awaited day finally arrives for you to meet with your contact, dress in your best business attire (see Chapter 6 for more on this) and arrive a few minutes early, so that you have adequate time to adjust your hair, tie or dress. Then take a deep breath and try to relax in the reception area before you are called. It will help to remember two things:

Your First Interview

1. This is *not* a job interview. This takes the pressure off both you and your contact. This meeting is simply an opportunity for you to gather information and, possibly a reference. Of course in the process, you will become *known* to your contact, so that when a new opportunity does happen to arise, you may be just the person who comes to mind.

2. *You* are in charge of the interview. You are the one who will be posing most of the questions.

When you finally get to meet your contact, greet him or her warmly and express your gratitude for this opportunity. Your meeting should go something like this:

You: *Thanks for taking time out of your busy schedule to meet with me, Ms. Burns. I've heard and read a lot about you.*

Contact: *Not at all. Dan Hyman and I go way back and he told me that you were really going places. I hope I can help. I think my secretary told you we have a hiring freeze on right now.*

You: *Yes. I've read about how hard the hotel industry was hit by the recession. But things seem to be turning around now. Am I right?*

C: *Yes, but slowly. The building boom has stopped, of course. And business people are starting to travel again. Our company came through this okay. We're beginning to experience a turnaround.*

Y: *Ms. Burns, I wanted to see you to ask you some questions that will help me get started in the hotel business. I've always wanted to work in the travel field and my studies at Howard Johnson's have convinced me that sales and marketing is the area I want to be in. Where's the best place for me to get my start?*

C: *Well, you'll have to start in sales or public relations. Hotels are fairly unsophisticated about marketing. People with marketing in their title often started out in the sales department of a single hotel. That's how I got my start.*

Y: *Should I apply to chain headquarters or to the individual properties to land an entry-level sales job?*

C: *Both. However, most of the junior sales positions are filled at the property level. If I were you, I'd try some of the larger convention properties that have large sales forces, like the Holiday Regency downtown here.*

Y: *Should I expect to be doing telephone sales for a while?*

C: *Yes. Then, if you perform well, you'll be given a "territory," such as religious conventions or travel agents, to call on.*

Y: *What entry-level salary should I expect?*

C: *Somewhere in the low 20s. We're starting people off at $23,000 when we have the rare position to fill.*

Y: *Are some areas of the country better than others in terms of job availability?*

C: *Right now, it's the older cities. Everyone wants to be in the Sun Belt and resort destinations. Las Vegas is one city where the hotel business is always healthy.*

Y: *I've also thought about joining an advertising agency that specializes in the hotel business. Can you name some of them?*

The interview proceeds like this for some time. Your contact has become comfortable, having by now realized that you're not here to harass her into hiring you. The questions have made her forget that this is, after all, a thinly disguised job interview. She gives you a lot of solid information, the names of some advertising agencies and hoteliers to contact—and permission to use her name when you do so. You diligently write these down.

In the meantime, you have made a favorable impression on her by demonstrating that you know the hotel industry and some of its key players. You also have demonstrated that you are a job candidate who really knows what you want in your career and you're doing your best to land a good position.

After the interview

The very day of the interview, dash off letters of thanks both to your contact and the person who referred you to her. Include a copy of your resume in the letter to your new contact, requesting that she pass it on to anyone looking for a qualified entry-level candidate.

Then, start the networking process all over again with the names you acquired from the informational interview. One of these is bound to land you a *real* job interview, the subject of the next chapter.

Chapter 5

Not the Spanish Inquisition!

What to expect during your first interview

For employers, interviewing has made the transition from art to science.

A long-time subscriber to journals for personnel executives, I've lately seen a plethora of articles extolling the virtues of such things as "database interviews," "situational interviews" and "stress (confrontational) interviews."

While these techniques each have their own nuances, they have been developed with one goal in mind: to more accurately and reliably measure how a candidate will perform on the job if hired.

Test-tube babies

Like scientists, interviewers are now expected to gather similar types of information on all the specimens they study: information that can be measured, quantified and more easily and accurately compared. In fact, sometimes it seems as if *quantification* has replaced *qualification* in the hiring process.

The reasons are not as much Orwellian as economic. The *cost of hire*, the amount of money it takes to land a suitable candidate for a job, has escalated dramatically and will continue to increase as a result of the baby bust and the much ballyhooed shrinkage of the work force.

In addition, lawsuits against employers for wrongful discharge and other employment-related causes have increased exponentially over the past decade, making it more important for companies to hire people whom they are fairly certain they won't want to get rid of.

And, last but not least, for companies in our new service economy, the "human" resource is unquestionably the most valuable in their inventories.

Translation:
Interviews will be tougher

Not to make you more nervous than you probably are already, but for all of these reasons, interviewing is going to get tougher and tougher for job candidates at all levels of experience. You probably will have to go through more interviews than your predecessors—no matter what job you're after or what your level of expertise. You may also have to endure a battery of tests designed to measure your honesty, intelligence, mental health and blood toxicity.

You're most likely to face the newest, toughest interview techniques on your interviews with staffers in the human resources (HR) departments. (They are usually the only ones who have read about these new techniques.)

While interviews with hiring managers are the "make or break" of the job-hunting process, you'll have to get ready for the difficult interviews with HR to get past first base.

Armed with these new interviewing techniques, HR staffers are better equipped than ever to select promising candidates before the hiring manager ever meets them.

The screening interview

If you are going for a job at a mid-sized or large company (any organization of more than about 250 employees), your first interview will often be with an employment or staffing manager in the HR department.

More and more often, this interview is taking candidates by surprise. Why? Because many companies have begun conducting the initial screening interview by phone in an effort to save time and/or do more with less staff.

Therefore, since this will probably not be scheduled in advance, you must begin preparing for the telephone interview as soon as you send out your resumes and letters.

"I'll get it."

The scene could go something like this: You're sitting at home having your orange juice on a warm summer day three weeks after graduation. The phone rings. You saunter over to answer it, casting sidelong glances at the headlines on the morning newspaper and scratching your stomach.

Your First Interview

"Hello," you groan.

"Good morning," says the almost too chipper voice on the other end. "This is Molly Ackroyd of ABC Widget. I'm looking for Joseph Lerman."

"Speaking."

"Oh, hello. May I call you Joseph? You applied for our opening in the solid waste management department, and I'm calling to ask you some preliminary questions."

You're about to freeze. You gulp almost audibly. Your head swims in a rush of adrenaline. You begin looking for a way out. You consider saying, "O-O-Oh, you want *Joseph* Lerman. I'm afraid he's not here right now. Can I take a message?"

But you think better of it. And it's a good thing. After all, on the other end of the phone is a recruiter for ABC Widget. Let's take a look at who she is and why she's calling you.

Just the facts

Molly is a lower-level person in the HR department who has been trained in some fairly basic interview techniques. Odds are that she hasn't been out of college much longer than you, and she has only a bare-bones idea of the duties and responsibilities of the position for which you've applied.

Her job has a rather simple goal: to reduce the number of *bona fide* candidates for an opening before any of them get a chance to even walk in the door.

After you've gotten through the preliminaries with Molly, her end of the conversation will follow a script. She will be asking questions to see if you have the *easily quantifiable* qualifications for the position—the right degree, command of the English language, the right types of internships or other experience, willingness to relocate, whatever.

Primarily, Molly will be trying to determine if you've been truthful on your resume.

The interview will also be somewhat qualitative: How well have you responded to her surprise phone call? And how quickly did you recover from the shock? Do you exhibit sufficient enthusiasm for the position? Do you exhibit any obvious emotional disturbances? How articulate are you? How energetic? How prepared? Should she or anybody else at Widget go out on a limb and actually recommend you for a job?

Take a deep breath—and smile! The first thing to do—and you'll have only a fraction of a second to do it—is to manage your anxiety. Since you are new to the job-hunting process, some nervousness at a time like this is perfectly normal. So, before answering Ms. Ackroyd, take a *deep* breath and slowly exhale as you respond to the call.

"Oh, Ms. Ackroyd, I'm so glad you called. What can I do for you this morning?"

Now, smile. Although Ms. Ackroyd can't see you, your smile will automatically make your voice sound more enthusiastic—this is a trick taught to all telephone salespeople and customer-service employees. In addition, form a mental picture of Ms. Ackroyd. Conjure up someone pleasant and nonthreatening and imagine that she's the person you're talking to. And don't forget to breathe between sentences.

Your First Interview

Your first response already has shown enthusiasm and a willingness to be cooperative. Since Molly might have 25 of these calls to make today, she'll be very grateful to you for making her job easier and more pleasant.

Remember, the telephone interview is a screening-out, not a screening-in process. Molly is trying to reduce the number of in-person interviews she, her supervisor and the hiring manager must conduct.

In other words, Molly desperately wants to scratch 24 of the 25 candidates she calls today off her list. The following tips can help you beat these odds.

- Make it easy for Molly to get hold of you or leave messages. Buy an answering machine if there is any time during business hours that your phone might not be answered.

- Be cheerful and enthusiastic without being phony about it. Remember to smile while you're speaking on the phone.

- Be prepared. Keep by the telephone a copy of your resume and cover letter and some basic facts about ABC Widget and the other companies you've applied to.

- Stay in control. If you don't have documents near the phone, if you're in your underwear and the doorbell has just rung, ask Molly to hold on a few seconds or offer to call her right back. Do it calmly and don't think you'll put her off. She knows she's caught you by surprise.

- Buy yourself some extra time to think by rephrasing Molly's questions and repeating them back to her. (Just don't repeat them verbatim. You'll sound as annoying as a parrot.) For example:

Molly: *"Please tell me a little bit about your internship at XYZ Dump."*

You: *"Ah, my internship last summer at XYZ? That was a terrific experience for me. I learned a great deal about solid waste management. For instance..."*

This is a means of "warming up" for your reply, or remembering those answers I hope you have rehearsed before now (see Chapter 7). It is also another way for you to calm yourself down and keep that natural anxiety from turning the interview into a natural disaster.

- Make sure to ask for the correct spelling of Molly's name, her complete title and the address of the company office she works in. You should follow up the telephone interview with a letter thanking her for calling and reaffirming your interest in the position.

- Don't volunteer anything. The telephone interviewer is out to get facts and assess the truthfulness of your application. If you volunteer something more, you might inadvertently give her a reason to reject you. If you abruptly switched majors, entered and left graduate school, resigned from an internship or part-time job, let Molly ask before you tell. Tell the truth when she does ask, but don't feel the need to unburden yourself if she doesn't.

The live and in-person screening interview

Let's face it, the deck is stacked against you when Molly calls. She wants to speak once and only once to as many people that day as possible. It's more difficult to put your best foot forward over the telephone. And, if the company is not in a remote location, it probably is using telephone screening because so many apparently qualified candidates applied for the position. Yes, that's right. You're not the only one to hear about that terrific job at ABC Widget. In fact, in this market you're most likely one of 500 applicants!

On the other hand, the live screening interview gives you a better chance to make a good impression (we'll discuss that more in the next chapter), and probably is an indication that there's a relatively small cadre of candidates or that your application is held in at least relatively high regard.

That's the good news. The bad news is that the live, and usually longer, interview gives Molly the chance to use all of the interview techniques she's learned and practiced.

She'll also have a chance to pass judgment on more than your words and the sound of your voice. She'll be, as the pessimists might put it, watching you squirm.

Get your emotions under control

So that you don't squirm too much, you must work at getting your emotions under control before the interview with Ms. Ackroyd begins. In order to do that:

1. **Arrive early.** If your appointment is at 9 a.m., aim to arrive at the building by 8:30, so you won't get overly flustered about finding the building or being late. If you're from out of town, consider arriving the night before for any interview—even if it means paying for an inexpensive hotel.

2. **Freshen up.** Proceed to the reception area 15 to 20 minutes before the scheduled start of the interview. Tell the receptionist that you are there to see Ms. Ackroyd, but that you would first like to visit the restroom. Take that opportunity to wash your hands and make sure that your hair and clothing are all in order. Look to see that there are no scuff marks on your shoes. If there are, get a paper towel and do your best to re-shine them. Looking spiffy? Good. It's time to meet Molly.

The trained interviewer's arsenal

Let's take a look at the techniques that Molly will use once you've passed muster over the telephone. Remember, she is trained and practiced in the science of interviewing to a degree that has probably never been even dreamed of by the hiring manager—the person you're hoping to work for (unless of course you're applying for a job in the HR department). And it is the hiring manager, you know, who will really decide if you'll be walking to work or still walking the pavement next week. Nevertheless, Molly Ackroyd is the gatekeeper. So it's just as important to impress her.

Your First Interview

You must get past her to get to the less scientific selection interview that will be conducted by your boss-to-be.

Let's start with what is, for most candidates, the worst possible test.

The stress interview

Anyone who's been through one of these never forgets it. The stress interview, becoming increasingly common these days, is designed to get past the pleasantries and under the veneer to see what the candidate is really made of.

I was subjected to a stress interview before I'd ever heard of the technique—not the best way to prepare, believe me—the worst possible scenario for any candidate.

Some years ago, I applied for an editorial position at a major publishing company and made it past the first hurdle, a screening interview conducted in the corporate office.

Next, I was invited to come back to meet the director of personnel. She greeted me pleasantly and led me back to her rather palatial office. We exchanged a few more pleasantries as I took my seat and settled in.

Before I knew it, I felt as if I were undergoing a police interrogation in a country cited frequently for human rights violations.

Assuming that I had been spoken of highly by the screening interviewer, I was shocked when she began questioning my credentials, sarcastically soliciting the reasons I had majored in liberal arts rather than something "practical," and asking me what in the world made me think that I could edit a magazine, even though I had been doing just that for years.

The interviewer's questions were fired quickly, and each successive question veered dizzyingly to a completely unrelated topic. One question would be about my work experience; the next, about what I did to stay fit; the next, about my favorite movie.

Her questions did exactly what I later learned they were intended to do—they made me feel confused, fearful and hostile. I behaved badly, answered as many questions as I could in monosyllables and avoided looking my inquisitor in the eye.

Needless to say, I was not offered the job.

How to ace a stress interview

I began our discussion of the interviewing process with a description of this technique because it emphasizes some very important lessons about all interviews:

- Stay calm no matter how stressful the situation. When the interviewer finishes asking a question, take a few seconds to compose yourself and your answer.

- Recognize the situation for what it is—an artificial scenario designed to see how you react under pressure. The interviewer (probably) has nothing against you personally.

- Don't let the interviewer get under your skin. It's easy to think that the interviewer has taken a strong dislike to you and that your chances are nil. That's not the case. The stress interview is designed to see if you will become depressed, hostile or flustered when the going gets tough.

- Watch your tone of voice. It's easy to become sarcastic during a stress interview because, presuming you don't realize what the interviewer is up to, you'll assume he or she has gone ballistic.

The structured or database interview

Much more common nowadays is what has come to be known as the structured or database interview. Although this might sound complicated or highly technological, both terms refer only to the fact that the interviewer must be careful to ask the same comprehensive set of questions of all candidates.

By asking exactly the same set of questions of every candidate, the theory goes, the interviewer will be able to accurately and fairly compare them. In other words, it allows the hiring organization to establish a complete database on each candidate (the term has nothing to do with computers, although computers might be used to store, retrieve and organize the data gathered) so that eventually it's comparing "apples to apples."

The structured interview can be conducted by more than one person. You will notice interviewers in these situations referring to a long list of questions, checking off things or writing out summaries of your answers.

Because of its comprehensiveness, the structured interview will drain you. You must be prepared to answer questions about your education, related experiences, personal likes and dislikes, interpersonal skills, management skills, if you've supervised other people and just about anything else connected to your skills, personality, experience and "potential."

If you haven't reviewed your personal inventory sheets prior to this type of interview, you will be unable to answer a number of questions about yourself—a situation guaranteed to make you look and feel pretty stupid.

The targeted interview

The targeted interview is narrower in scope, with nearly all of the questions designed to mine information about the specific skills the employer has deemed necessary for success on the job available.

During a targeted interview for a sales position in a remote office, for instance, you might be asked many questions about your interpersonal skills, your self-discipline and the degree to which you procrastinate.

The problem with this type of interview for the candidate is that only a part of the "real you" is given the chance to shine through. You might have several strengths that mitigate a weakness in one area, but the interview might not give you the chance to demonstrate them.

How to ace a structured or targeted interview

- Keep your answers terse, but thorough. You might hope that the interviewer asks you about different parts of your background, but don't talk about areas the interviewer doesn't ask about. The interviewer in a structured format wants you to give him the facts—and only the facts that he or she is asking about.

- Be prepared to answer many questions about just one part of your background or personality. The company has deemed this area an important one for your success.

The situational interview

"Let's suppose everyone but you called in sick and..." Questions like this will tell you that you are in the midst of the increasingly popular situational interview.

Like the targeted interview, the situational interview is geared toward measuring the degree to which candidates demonstrate traits deemed key for success in a given position.

The interviewer elicits this information by posing a series of real or hypothetical situations and asking how the candidate would act in each one.

Usually companies are trying to measure candidates' resourcefulness, logic, conceptual thinking ability, creativity and logical thinking.

How to ace a situational interview

Situational interviews allow candidates to really shine if they:

- Avoid the bull. No type of interview technique invites candidates to be boastful, to exaggerate or to downright fabricate more than the situational interview. But no other technique exposes that tendency in a candidate so effectively.

  Show that you have a grasp of the real world and that you realize you have a lot to learn about the business. This will be much more effective than trying to act like Donald Trump.

- Think through your answers. "You're faced with a production deadline and several people in your department have called in sick..." "Your biggest customer says he's tired of having the company change salesmen on him and he's taking all of his business to a competitor..." These kinds of hypothetical situations are as complex as real life. Before you glibly announce that you'd just hire temps or make reservations at the city's best restaurant, think about possible results and repercussions of your decisions.

Theory why

It is not the purpose of this book to frighten you. But forewarned, as they say, is forearmed.

Your First Interview

As someone with little or no experience, you represent something of a conundrum for human resource professionals. They are well-schooled in interview theory, and the belief that holds sway in the field is that "past performance and behavior are the single most reliable factors known in predicting future performance and behavior" (according to Richard H. Beatty, president of the Bradford Group, an executive search firm).

Given the fact that you have no experience, you don't fit in with the basic theory of interviews. Zealous screening interviewers, therefore, will be trying to ferret out information about your college performance, your personality and your personal, interactive style that will be predictive of "future performance."

As a new kid on the block, you are making their job a little more difficult to do well, or to do as scientifically. They might not like that, and might be more tempted to try out hypothetical questions, stress techniques and other means to get at the real you.

A track record would obviate the need for this type of performance test.

It's downhill from here...sort of

This might seem awfully complicated. But remember, human resources professionals are usually the only people at a company trained in sophisticated interviewing techniques. However, the interview with the hiring manager, as we will see in the next chapter, has its own challenges and opportunities for you to demonstrate why you're the best person for the job.

Chapter 6

Walk right in, sit right down

You don't get a second chance to make a first impression

If there's one notion that all interviewers share, it's that you, as a candidate, are giving them your very best shot. They are convinced that what they see and hear during the interview—the way you're dressed, the degree of politeness you exhibit, your demeanor, your social skills—are the best you've got.

After all, you're trying to convince a total stranger that he or she should invest substantial amounts of time and money in you. Why wouldn't you look and act your best?

Now, I'm sure some of you think you look best in a Hawaiian shirt and cutoffs, and you might be right, but a job interview is one time in your life when it's probably best to put aside individuality in your choice of wardrobe.

This is the one chapter in which I can tyrannically say that there is only one right way to do things. In discussing how you should dress for an interview, I feel entirely comfortable throwing impartiality and individualism out the window. Once you're in the interview, you will be playing the interviewer's game. If you want the job, you must play by his or her rules.

How men should dress for the interview

There is no magic or imagination required to pick out the best outfit a man should wear on a job interview—just make like Betsy Ross and think red, white, and blue. Red tie, white shirt, blue suit.

Invest now in a navy blue wool, wool-worsted or wool-blend suit. It will look better and last longer than a suit made of other fabrics, and it will go with almost anything. Select a single-breasted, two-piece fashion, preferably vented.

This might sound old-fashioned, but for most jobs, the best bet is to dress conservatively, with minimal flash. Your shirt should be long-sleeved, professionally starched and pressed (it's well-worth the buck or two), and reveal no fraying at the collar or cuffs. Button-down Oxford or spread collars are best.

Your tie should be a silk foulard in a subdued red with a stripe or small pattern in the same blue as your suit. This will add a bit of subtle personal expression to your ensemble.

Remember that you should not wear any pins, cuff links or ties that bear a religious or service affiliation (unless you want to make your outside affiliation a basis for your cmployment). Why risk turning an interviewer off?

One possible exception might arise if you discover through your research that you share a common affiliation with your interviewer. In this a case, for example, wearing a subtle Masonic pin might make a positive impression on an interviewer who's a Mason. The danger, even in this case, is that you will so impress the interviewer that he or she will bring you around to meet some other people who *don't* share that affiliation. In general, it's better to avoid the outer display. If you've discovered something you have in common, simply work it into your conversation in a diplomatic and natural way.

Your watch should not be a Swatch or other stylish plastic make, but a conservative model with a stretch metal or leather band—it needn't be expensive.

Wear black or navy blue socks that cover your entire calf. If you cross your legs during the interview, you don't want any of your rugby injuries to show.

And don't forget to polish your shoes. They should be black, conservative loafers or lace-ups with a low heel.

How women should dress for the interview

As you'll notice throughout your career, women have a great deal more flexibility than men in their choice of business attire. However, the greater number of options doesn't imply complete freedom in the interview situation.

Women must take care to avoid what could be considered provocative clothing—V-neck sweaters, short skirts or patterned stockings, for example. They should wear dresses or suits in muted colors and non-shiny fabrics, such as wool.

Women should also avoid large, clunky or noisy fashion jewelry, oversized hand-bags, open-toed shoes and spike heels. You'll want to look much more like Murphy Brown than Julia Roberts did in the opening scene of *Pretty Woman*.

Unisex grooming for success

There are several grooming rules that apply to both sexes:

- **Don't overdo the perfume or cologne.** It's not that you shouldn't wear perfume or cologne, but don't wear so much your "essence" will linger in the room for the rest of the week.

- **Carry a slim, easy-to-carry leather folder.** It should be large enough to hold a few copies of your resume and a small notebook.

- **Pay attention to hygiene and grooming.** Your hair (including mustaches and beards, men), should be neatly trimmed. Avoid excessive hair spray and, if possible, the types of hairstyles that would require it. Make sure that your fingernails are clean and clipped. Women should avoid dark red nail polish. And don't have any spicy foods on the way to the appointment.

   If you smoke, avoid doing so prior to the interview. A greater number of workplaces are "smoke-free" these days. Therefore, the smell of smoke will indicate that you might have a problem following an important company policy.

Watch your (body) language

You'll have so much to think about during the interview that you might very well overlook what your body is up to. I watched a candidate pick at a mole during an entire 45-minute interview, oblivious to how uncomfortable this might make even the most stout-hearted (and strong-stomached) interviewer, of which I was not one. Here are some tips that will keep your body from betraying you.

Hands off!

When you get to the reception area, take off your coat and hat and hang them in a closet, if one is available. This will ensure that you have one less thing to fumble with later on. If you are in the reception area for a while, keep your hands exposed, not in your pockets. This will keep them from getting too clammy.

When the interviewer comes to meet you, extend your hand, look him or her straight in the eye and offer a greeting. Make sure that your handshake is firm, but not crushing, and don't worry about your palms being a little damp. Most interviewers understand that this is not an easy moment for any candidate.

Follow the interviewer into his or her office. This is a good time to make some small talk. "My, these offices are beautiful! How long have you been at this address?" Or, "We're lucky to have such cool weather in August (or such warm weather in November)."

Remember, try to keep your conversation positive. It's a bad idea to start off with something like, "Boy, I can't stand this muggy weather" or "I thought I would never find this place!" You may prompt the interviewer to think, at least on a subconscious level, that you're a negative person or that you secretly wish you were somewhere else.

Sitting pretty

As you enter the interviewer's office, wait for his or her cue as to where you should sit if there is more than one obvious choice. If you are offered any chair, choose the one closest to and directly opposite the interviewer's chair. This will demonstrate your confidence.

Don't immediately begin rooting around in your folder for your resume. Make a little bit more small talk to help you—and the interviewer—ease into the Q & A.

Again, the conversational icebreaker should be fairly innocuous, but upbeat. "How many employees do you have here at headquarters?" "This part of the state sure has seen a lot of development recently, hasn't it?"

If you are seated at a table, interlock your fingers and keep your hands on the tabletop. This will keep you from fidgeting. If seated on a chair or couch, keep your feet flat on the floor (don't cross your legs), keep your hands in your lap and interlock your fingers.

This is not to say that you shouldn't talk with your hands if you're like me and do so quite naturally. Be yourself—but when you're not using your hands to make a point, it's best to keep them folded and still.

Make eye contact throughout the entire interview, but don't overdo it. You're not engaged in a staring contest with Clint Eastwood. And staring without pause at the interviewer will not make his day.

Be aware of your body. Take care not to slouch. You may appear lazy or sloppy. On the other hand, don't sit there like a marine at attention. You're likely to seem edgy and overly aggressive—a real "Type A" personality.

Are you nervous?

If you have a pulse, of course you are! The interview is a difficult situation, but you can't allow nervousness to make you freeze. Here are some additional tips on relaxing so that you'll be at your best during the interview (also look over the tips in Chapter 5):

- **Take a deep breath.** In fact, take several while you're waiting for the interviewer to greet you. This will help stem the natural "fight-or-flight" response we all experience when we're anxious. Deep breathing helps even the worst phobics control their fears. It's an effective way to overcome the physiological causes of panic.

- **Do a last-minute check.** Make sure that your resume is readily available in your folder. Then, pick up a magazine and read the most meaningless article you can find. But avoid newspapers, since the newsprint probably will come off on your sweaty palms.

- **Think about what you're here to learn.** The interviewer is not the only one seeking information. You have come to this interview to find out more about the company. So think of yourself as an important participant in the interview, not just one of many interchangeable candidates to be studied as if you were a specimen on a slide. In fact, *you* will be in charge of some parts of the interview. So get ready to speak up.

Think of the interview as an adventure, as a learning experience, as a chance to brag about yourself and actually (or hopefully) get rewarded for it.

Don't get off to a bad start

All of this advice is fairly easy to remember. Your choice of wardrobe is limited. And you have to remember to be enthusiastic, polite and calm.

However, following the advice can be a bit more difficult when your heart is beating like mad as you head to the interviewer's office.

Practice deep breathing—that's right, practice it—so that it comes easily and automatically when stress begins to set in.

And have one of your friends or relatives play the role of the Grand Inquisitor so you can rehearse how you will act during the interview.

If you have access to the equipment, videotape a role-play interview. You'll notice little tics and habits that you might be able to control so they don't distract the interviewer from the *you* underneath that nice blue suit.

Now that you're well-dressed and ready, let's get on to the real thing.

Chapter 7

Here there be dragons

Your interview with the hiring manager

Right now you're probably thinking, "Hey, I'll be doing really well if I make it past the screener in the human resources department who has been trained in this interviewing stuff. The hiring manager probably doesn't know as much about interviewing, so getting past him will be a piece of cake."

Wrong!

Skilled interviewers—those conducting the screening interviews—have had ample experience with the interview process. They are ready with a set of questions. And unless you turn them off in the first few minutes, they will proceed to ask each one.

They know how to stay in charge of an interview, not let it meander down some dead-end sidetrack.

And they usually won't ask any questions that they are not legally permitted to ask.

In other words, they know what they're doing and how to do it. And they are confident in their skills and knowledge. Ironically, this makes them *easier* to interview with than hiring managers.

Almost surely, hiring managers will lack some or all of the screening interviewers' knowledge, experience and interviewing skill. Therefore, they pose a much greater challenge. The hiring manager is more likely to ask open-ended questions, more likely to lose control of the interview and more prone to meander. In many ways, you'll be on your own, in uncharted waters, much like the early explorers sailing into territory noted on maps as "Here there be dragons."

Your goal during the interview with the hiring manager is to inspire his or her confidence in you. That means you will have to be more prepared.

Flying by the seat of their pants

Why are hiring managers, for the most part, inferior interviewers? The reason is that very few managers in corporate America actually know what it takes to hire the right candidate. Most of them have never had formal training in conducting an interview.

What's more, most managers conducting interviews are only slightly more comfortable than the candidates sitting opposite them.

I got a feeling

Remember what I said in Chapters 1 and 2 about knowledge equaling confidence? Well, hiring managers lack confidence, or possess only false confidence, about their ability to conduct a penetrating, conclusive interview.

Why is the hiring manager's scant knowledge of interviewing potentially dangerous to you? Well, it can mean that he or she will decide you are not the best candidate after asking vague questions or even *wrong* questions. In other words, the person who interviews you might make a hiring decision based on factors that have virtually little or nothing to do with you or your actual qualifications!

Just as the screening interviewer is looking for a set of facts that will help him or her give candidates a "pass" or "fail" grade, the hiring manager is looking for insights into the personality of the candidate.

He or she is looking for just enough information to allow intuition to take over. In other words, facts are often not the goal. The hiring manager is looking for a candidate he or she can feel good about hiring. That places the focus of the interview not only on your measurable skills, but on something much more subjective—his or her sense of whether you are likely to be a good "organizational fit."

Of course some hiring managers are skilled interviewers. These are the people who will use techniques like the situational interview to get a sense of how a candidate will perform on the job. Those who lack skills (the majority) tend to be much more passive. Many are secretly hoping that the candidate will do a certain "something" during the interview that will be the equivalent of saying, "Hey, I'm the one for you."

In this chapter, the most important in the book, I'll discuss how to inspire the hiring manager's confidence in you, how to field questions like, "So, tell me about yourself," and how to know when it's appropriate for you to seize control of the interview.

Inspiring confidence

At one time, I was trying to fill two production positions at my publishing company. I had just decided to install desktop publishing, a technology that was at that time still in its infancy, so I was looking for candidates who knew something about basic book production, of course—but who could also show me they had the ability and willingness to learn about this new technology.

As a result, my hiring criteria were much more vague than usual. Into this situation walked Eric. He had a small amount of experience in journal publishing, and even less experience using computers for anything at all. But I hired him. What convinced me to hire him was his enthusiasm.

He was so interested in learning desktop publishing that he couldn't stop asking questions about it. He'd already read a good deal about it and could talk about its intricacies for hours. Eric exhibited a great deal of confidence and demonstrated that he was not only excited to learn about the new technology, but convinced that he could.

Hiring Eric paid off. Despite his lack of experience, he took to desktop publishing like the proverbial fish to water—learning it with such rapidity that within one year I put him in charge of coordinating repairs, buying equipment and evaluating new software packages.

The lesson for *you* in this story is that confidence and enthusiasm are probably the two key things that a hiring manager is looking for. I think that even if Eric had had no experience in production, I'd have hired him because he demonstrated such an overwhelming willingness to learn and work hard.

Putting out the right vibes

How can you convey your confidence and enthusiasm to a hiring manager? Here are some tips:

- **Think of the interview as an adventure.** I know that might sound strange, but you *can* make even the toughest interview an enjoyable experience if you display enthusiasm and get the hiring manager interested in you.

  One friend of mine, who was considering going to law school, took the LSATs while he was making up his mind. He scored pretty badly, so he signed up to take them again. By the time the next test date rolled around, he'd decided to pursue another career option.

  He went ahead and took the LSATs again anyway, thinking of them as an experience, an adventure. Besides, he wanted to see how well he could do. This time he doubled his score! He certainly hadn't prepared more. But his attitude about taking the test was right. *Because he felt no pressure* or anxiety, his mind was allowed to perform at its best.

- **Be polite.** You may need to be tactful during the interview. For instance, if the interviewer says something offensive to you, don't jump down his or her throat. Just pause a moment and say something like, "Well, I know many people feel that way, but I think..." In other words, be a diplomat.

- **Be enthusiastic.** About the position, about your accomplishments, about what you've found out about the company. I remember one candidate who sat like a bump on a log throughout an interview for a junior editorial position. She asked no questions and gave only terse replies to mine. I cut the interview short because I felt she didn't want the job. I was shocked when she repeatedly called to see if I'd made my final choice. It turned out that she *desperately* wanted the position. She certainly didn't convey that to me when it really *counted*.

- **Keep on smiling.** A smile makes you appear agreeable and pleasant. And who wouldn't want to work with a pleasant and agreeable person like you? Sure, you're accustomed to giving people a big smile when you shake hands with them. But it's also important to keep smiling at appropriate places during the interview. Your smiles should be natural, spontaneous and most of all sincere. Just don't let a smile freeze on your face until you begin to look a little deranged.

- **Make eye contact.** Have you ever known someone who wouldn't look you in the eye? Eventually you begin to wonder what that person has to hide. Make eye contact while you're shaking hands with the interviewer and periodically throughout the interview. However, you should avoid staring or making continuous eye contact—that would make anyone feel uncomfortable.

- **Be honest.** Express enthusiasm only about the things you are truly enthusiastic about. Phoniness will not sell the hiring manager on you.

- **Be positive.** It's best to keep negative words out of your interview vocabulary. Let's say you switched majors and the interviewer asks why. Don't say, "I couldn't stand the professors in the economics department. I just had to get out of there." Instead, try something like, "I got a lot out of studying economics, but I became absolutely fascinated with marketing, so I decided to make the switch."

  As you're rehearsing your answers to interview questions, take all of the negative words out. And before you go into any interview, repeat this to yourself one thousand times: "Be positive!"

"So, tell me a little about yourself."

This is the favorite question of the trained interviewer, because it gives him or her the opportunity to study a host of reactions—from verbal cues to body language.

It is also a favorite of the untrained interviewer for quite a different reason—simply because he or she usually doesn't know what else to ask.

It's therefore a good idea to assume that this question will be put to you and to prepare for it the way presidential candidates prepare for televised debates—by developing and rehearsing a set reply. Otherwise, you may be fated to react like the narrator in essayist J. B. Priestly's piece, "All About Ourselves":

"Now tell me," said the lady, "all about yourself."
The effect was instantaneous, shattering. Up to that
moment, I had been feeling expansive; I was self-
confident, alert, ready to give a good account of
myself in the skirmish of talk. If I had been asked
my opinion of anything between here and Sirius, I
would have given it at length, and I was quite
prepared to talk of places I had never seen and
books I had never read; I was ready to lie, and to lie
boldly and well. Had she not made that fatal
demand, I would have roared.

When *you* are asked that "fatal" question, remember
the cardinal rule of interviewing: The hiring manager
wants to feel good about you. Your primary goal is to let
him or her do just that.

And there is a second rule: The hiring manager wants
you to make him or her feel confident that hiring you will
be a good decision. Your answer to this question should be
targeted to do just that.

Taking stock once again

To prepare an excellent answer to this question, look
back at the personal inventory I urged you to prepare in
Chapter 1. Most important in preparing your answer are
items you listed under the headings:

- Strongest skills.

- Greatest areas of knowledge.

- Strongest parts of personality.

- Things I do best.

- Key accomplishments.

Take that information and turn it into a speech of about 250 words (that would take less than one minute to speak). Here is a proposed outline of this brief verbal picture of you:

1. Key accomplishments.

2. Key strengths demonstrated by those accomplishments.

3. The importance of these accomplishments and strengths for the hiring manager.

Here's an example of a solid one-minute speech:

I fell in love with engineering in high school and have wanted to work in aerospace ever since. My internship at ABC Aircraft gave me a tremendous amount of experience on the drafting table and in the use of computer-aided engineering. ABC called me back for two subsequent summer internships.

I was a straight-A student in my major field of study, physics, and have a paper being considered for publication in the Journal of Metal Fatigue, *something, I'm told, that not many undergraduates have accomplished.*

Of course, I learned a great deal in college, but I think the greatest learning experience was at ABC. I realized the importance of being a self-starter, how to take initiative when I had ideas and how to get along with engineers with far more experience and knowledge than I.

I'm tremendously excited about the prospect of working at your company. I have admired its Airloft jet engine and the fact that you are continually at the forefront of the industry. I've also read a great deal about your computer-aided engineering and manufacturing systems and am excited about learning more about this technology.

Also, your policy of encouraging scientists and engineers to publish and win recognition in their fields fits in perfectly with my professional goals. While I think that working for a firm can be extremely rewarding, the greatest achievement for a scientist is the recognition of his peers.

Can you tell me, Mr. Smith, how the installation of CAD/CAM has improved the effectiveness of your department?

In this little speech, the interviewee has:

1. Bragged a bit about his grades and the area of his knowledge without getting carried away.

2. Shown that he knows the difference between college and the "real world" and recognizes the value of his experience in the latter.

3. Demonstrated a knowledge of the company's products and personnel policies.

4. Expressed enthusiasm for working at the company.

5. Talked about some of his personal strengths (ambition, the tendency to be a self-starter, the ability to learn new things quickly).

6. Taken temporary control of the interview at the end of his answer by asking Mr. Smith an informed question.

Not bad for a couple hundred words! Write your little speech on a piece of paper, rewrite it, rewrite it—then rewrite it again. You want it to sound natural and conversational, but to include all the key points you want to emphasize.

It should not have a lot of dependent clauses and tricky constructions, because people don't talk that way unless they've memorized a speech. You *don't* want to sound like Bob Hope reading from internal cue cards. That would certainly give the interviewer a bad impression. But if you have a speech like the one above, you'll knock him or her out.

Also, anticipate the questions the interviewer might ask after you give your speech about yourself and prepare answers for *those* questions. You certainly don't want to look as if you have nothing more to say after you've finished your canned presentation.

Taking control of the interview

Many candidates go into the interview thinking they are there for only one reason: to answer questions.

Nothing could be further from the truth. Yes, you are going to the interview for only one reason, but that reason is *to sell the interviewer on the fact that you are the best person for the job*.

You will do this by *giving* terrific answers to the interviewer's questions, by *asking* great questions about the company and the position and by *telling* the interviewer the things about yourself that you want him or her to know.

Let's say you went to an automobile showroom knowing just a little about a particular car. You are approached by an affable salesman who answers your questions but doesn't volunteer any information you hadn't asked about and asks no questions of you. Do you think you'd end up buying a car from him?

Most candidates approach the job interview like this hapless salesman. They are prepared to answer questions, but hesitate to volunteer information unless it's asked for—even if that information concerns some of their key talents or strengths.

Don't miss the opportunity to sell yourself. The fact that a customer walked into the showroom should have been enough to inspire that car salesman to do his best. Similarly, the fact that you've been called in for the interview has given you a chance to sell yourself. Don't blow it just because the interviewer doesn't ask the questions you were hoping he would. Find some means to give your answers anyway.

Standing apart from the crowd

At one company I worked for, a manager, Howard, ran a large and growing department. Consequently, he did a great deal of hiring.

The human resources department began to notice that he had the highest ratio of candidates interviewed to candidates hired of any manager at the company, and that many of the candidates that he turned down seemed absolutely terrific to everybody else. Finally, the human resources director asked one successful candidate what the interview with Howard had been like. The candidate said, "Well, it wasn't what I expected. He just talked to me about the company and the position for about 30 minutes and then asked me if I had any questions. I think I was lucky that I had a lot of good questions."

From that time on, the human resources director would tell people she considered to be leading candidates to "ask a lot of good questions during your interview with Howard."

The reason Howard employed his rather stilted interview technique was that he was a shy, introverted man. He happened to excel at certain important areas of his job, but interviewing certainly wasn't one of them.

Howard felt in complete command while he was talking about the company, but he had a great deal of trouble making even the smallest bit of small talk.

Therefore, only candidates who found some way to differentiate themselves, who took some initiative, would stand out in Howard's mind after the dozen or so interviews he might conduct to fill each opening.

Seize the day

Like Howard, many less-experienced interviewers often have a tendency to talk too much. In those situations, you must take charge—ask questions constantly.

If the interviewer has been speaking nonstop for 10 minutes when he says, "We've increased sales 20 percent every year for the past decade," politely interrupt with a question like, "That's very impressive in a mature industry like the bowling-pin spotting equipment market. How has the company maintained such growth?"

Talking faster doesn't help

At the opposite extreme is the interviewer who will let the poor candidate ramble on and on in answer to a single question because he has so few others to ask.

If you're faced with such a situation, be careful and watch how the interviewer is reacting to your soliloquy. If he exhibits what seems to be a negative response—crossing his arms across his chest, sitting bolt upright in his chair, fidgeting, tapping his fingers on the desk, shuffling papers—change the subject or ask him a question. You're not getting anywhere by continuing to flap your gums.

Don't make the mistake of talking faster once you notice his discomfort. You may be thinking this will help you get to whatever the interviewer really wants to hear faster. It's more likely that he just wants to hear his own voice for a minute or two!

I'll discuss interview behavior at greater length in Chapter 8. For now, just remember that the interview with the hiring manager is apt to be quite different from that with the personnel department.

Because the hiring manager is less experienced, the interview is probably going to present more of a challenge. But if you handle it correctly, it also presents a greater opportunity to allow your key strengths to shine through.

Again, I urge you to be prepared with a little speech about who you are, and to be ready to answer a far greater number of open-ended questions (starting with why and how, rather than who, what and where).

If you want to use your school experiences as a reference, think of the HR department interviews as the multiple-choice and true-or-false parts of an exam, while the hiring manager's interview is more like the essay section. You have to know the facts for both, but the second requires you to explain the implications of those facts.

Also remember that, unlike the screening interviewer, the hiring manager's primary goal in an interview is to establish not a set of facts, but a feeling. He or she wants to feel confident that you are the best person for the job. Don't let a lack of preparation or a hesitancy to speak up keep you from a job you want and deserve.

Chapter 8

You, in the spotlight

The finer points of interviewee technique

Until now, I've discussed, in broad strokes, how you should conduct yourself during the interview. In this chapter, I'll present some of the finer points that will help you score big when you meet with the HR department or the hiring manager.

I know that it seems as if you already have a lot to think about, but some of the lessons in this chapter will really help you stand out from the crowd of candidates.

Demonstrate an interest in the interviewer

Surprisingly enough, interviewers *are* human (for the most part). Like you, they respond positively to people who demonstrate a genuine interest in them. And they become impatient or bored with people who seem too self-absorbed.

Therefore, you can score big points if you demonstrate an interest in the interviewer. This is particularly true if the interview is with the hiring manager. After all, he or she is looking for an individual whose mission will be to help him, someone who will be attentive and responsive.

Showing an interest in the interviewer will go a long way toward convincing the hiring manager that you will care about his or her needs and goals after you're hired.

Out on a limb

A friend of mine landed a prime position at a brand-new company launched by a legendary entrepreneur in his industry. He was selected over many good candidates for this plum position. This was a triumph for my friend, especially since this entrepreneur, whom I'll call Larry, was known to be difficult to impress.

My friend, Cameron, told this story about the interview:

Here was Larry, a multimillionaire, sitting with a secretary and one other employee in this nearly empty 10,000 square feet of office shell. They had lights, a phone, a postage machine, some furniture and that's about it. There were workmen off in one corner, building some walls for his office.

Naturally, I was expecting a little more, and somehow these strange circumstances completely wiped away my nervousness. When Larry stood up to greet me, I introduced myself, then said, "I bet it has been a long time since you opened your own mail." At first, I couldn't believe I had done that, but Larry laughed and off we went.

For the next hour, Cameron had a ball talking with Larry about the launch of what promised to be an exciting company. He stayed loose during the entire interview, realizing that his going out on a limb had paid off. He felt—and expressed—enthusiasm for the utter lack of structure at the new company and said, "Larry really picked up on that. I could sense his violent dislike for big structures, so I took pains to stress *my* preference for lean, mean companies."

Cameron's move was risky. In this case, it worked because it displayed confidence, it implied a knowledge of Larry's background and it suggested that Cameron was aware that Larry wanted this company to grow to the point that a mailroom would make sense.

Controlling interest

Cameron had a great deal of control in the interview because he continued to demonstrate an interest in Larry's problems. In fact, in response to almost any of the challenges Larry discussed, Cameron had a question. He would ask, "How did that work?" or, "At ABC, we had a similar problem. Let me tell you briefly what worked."

Cameron came across as an interested, sympathetic problem-solver. He got an offer for the job that afternoon.

Granted, Cameron was presented with a golden interview opportunity. But he had the experience—and the *chutzpah*—to seize upon it and play it to the hilt.

Oh, sure you can!

You're probably saying, "But I can't do anything like *that*." Maybe not. It's not often that opportunities like the one Cameron had come along. What's more, you don't have the type of job experience you can draw on to wow an interviewer.

But you *can* display your interest in the interviewer with the simplest of comments: "I recognized you from your picture in the employee newsletter. Congratulations on your recent promotion." "Is that a Power Mac on your desk? I've heard great things about those machines. How do you like it?" "That's a wonderful photograph on your wall. Where was it taken?"

Don't overdo this. Nothing is worse than "smarminess," unless the interviewer is an egomaniac.

Build a vocabulary of positive action words

What? A vocabulary lesson for a 45-minute interview?

Granted, this might seem like overkill, but you'll use this vocabulary on your resume, in your job-hunting letters, during interviews, in your follow-up letters—and in every business letter you'll write for the rest of your life.

Always think in terms of positive, action words. They needn't be "five-dollar" words, but they should be words that stand out from normal conversational lingo. This list is just a sample, but you get the idea.

Here it is. Read it over every day. Build some of it into the little speech about yourself discussed in Chapter 7.

Action words

accomplished	edited	obtained
achieved	eliminated	operated
accelerated	established	ordered
administered	evaluated	organized
analyzed	examined	performed
approved	formulated	planned
arranged	founded	prepared
assisted	guided	presented
built	headed	produced
calculated	identified	provided
compiled	implemented	recommended
completed	improved	reduced
composed	increased	reorganized
conducted	initiated	replaced
consolidated	inspected	reported
consulted	installed	researched
controlled	instituted	reviewed
coordinated	instructed	revised
created	invented	scheduled
decreased	justified	selected
delivered	led	solved
designed	lectured	studied
developed	maintained	supervised
devised	managed	trained
directed	modified	translated
discovered	motivated	won
distributed	negotiated	wrote

Concentrate, concentrate, concentrate

Have you ever been in a conversation and realized that while you've been speaking, the person supposedly listening to you was thinking only about what he'd say next? You'd probably think that person was pretty self-centered and obviously uninterested in you and what you had to say.

Employers go one step further. They think that people demonstrating such behavior during a job interview are lacking one of the most important skills a good employee needs: the ability to listen, to be attentive, to react to the situation at hand.

During an interview, many candidates have a tendency to let their guard down after a certain amount of time. Oh, they start off enthusiastically and attentively, full of vim and vigor, but once they think they've gotten through the toughest part of the interview, they start to relax.

Don't do it. Don't get *too* relaxed. You should be concentrating on everything the interviewer says and asks so that you can formulate impressive questions and tell him precisely what he wants to know.

I know that you're at a time in your life when staying up late is the norm. But, before the big day of your job interview, pack it in early. Get plenty of rest so you're ready to face this big challenge alert and at your best.

I recommend that unless you have an adverse reaction to caffeine, have a cup or two of coffee or tea about 30 minutes before the interview so that your mind is sharp. Just don't overdo it—a fidgety caffeine overdose is hell to deal with during an interview!

Answer the question

After you give an answer, look your interviewer in the eye and prepare to listen, and I mean *listen*, to the next question. Then give him or her the appropriate answer.

If the interviewer asked for a specific set of facts, don't lose yourself in a mountain of details and conjure up all of the implications and explanations he or she didn't ask for.

Be terse and direct. You'll score more points. Long-winded answers will make the interviewer wish you'd leave and go bend some other manager's ear.

Now, wait a second

Many interviewees seem to be under the false assumption that they will score extra points during their interviews if they answer questions quickly. So, they begin speaking as soon as the interviewer finishes with the question, usually rushing headlong into an answer they soon wish they could revise or, worse yet, withdraw entirely!

It's a much better idea to allow for a short pause after the question so that you can compose a terrific answer.

What if a short pause is not enough? Then stall for more time with phrases like "Now, let me see," "I'm glad you asked that question." Or paraphrase the question:

Interviewer: *Tell me, what made you decide to change your major six times during your undergraduate days?*

Candidate: *Why did I change my major so often?*
Well, let me see, there were several
reasons while I was an underclassman,
but...

See? Without a lot of "umms" and "uhhs," the candidate has fairly successfully stalled for time.

No question is a throwaway

Some questions might seem unimportant, but don't ever treat them that way. Give equally careful consideration to every answer.

For instance, one acquaintance of mine thought that enthusiasm and a good work ethic should weigh more heavily in his consideration of candidates for most positions than their experience or education.

So many of the seemingly innocent questions he asked were designed to evaluate to what degree candidates possessed these characteristics. He asked about hobbies, believing that those without interests were either dull or lazy.

He'd also give careful consideration to candidates' comments about the weather, getting to the interview, the hectic days after college.

Candidates who consistently expressed negative views or started whining about these matters were not considered for hire.

So, be on your guard—remember that most employers are looking for enthusiasm, confidence, dependability and vigor.

If you whine your way through questions about the weather, you won't be thought of as someone possessing energy and the right attitude.

And if you point out that it took you hours to find the interviewer's office because you failed to get detailed directions, well, so much for your competence and dependability.

Be decisive

Open-ended questions are a double-edged sword. In Chapter 6, I urged you to prepare a little speech to deliver when you're asked, "How would you describe yourself?"

Well, there are a lot of other open-ended questions likely to come up: "What are your key strengths?" "What are your goals?" "What accomplishment are you most proud of?" "Why did you choose your major?" "Why do you want to relocate to our area?" "How would your best friend describe you?" You should have prepared the answers to these and similar kinds of questions.

Avoid the kinds of answers too many candidates give to these types of questions: "Boy, that's a tough one. Hmmm, I've never thought about that, but I guess if I had to choose one accomplishment, I would have to say that it might be making the dean's list seven straight semesters. Although I am really proud of my Eagle Scout pin. No, I'd have to say the dean's list. Definitely the Eagle Scout pin."

Such answers make candidates look indecisive—not exactly a trait employers are looking for. So, after pausing to consider your answer and stalling smoothly, hit the interviewer with your best shot—and stick with it.

Don't add, "Well, gee, maybe neither was really the one I'm most proud of. Maybe it's the fact that I earned a lot of my college expenses during my summers." Sure, you want to score that point, but wait for another opportunity.

The sound of silence

Nothing sounds worse for a stand-up comic than silence. Hence, the old line, "I know you're out there. I can hear you breathing," from the comedian desperate for a laugh.

If the silence starts to become deafening during your interview, you'll probably feel even more desperate. And that's just how some interviewers want you to feel. The most experienced inquisitors use silence to see how a candidate will squirm. And squirm they usually do!

A candidate confronted by interviewer silence will begin retracting what he just said, restate what he just said in slightly different words or begin volunteering more information than he should. Not helpful reactions.

Avoid doing any of these things. My best advice is the same given to every neophyte sales representative: "Once you've made the sale, shut up." (Granted, it's the lesson that takes most salespeople a lifetime to learn.)

Retracting, restating, muttering or launching into a complete history of your life when you're faced with interviewer silence will not help your image at all. It will make you appear indecisive.

Or, worse, it might lead you to say things you'd decided you wouldn't say during the interview—the less-than-rational reasons you switched majors, the fact that you hated your internships or the fact that you were rejected by seven graduate schools. When you are finished answering a question, *show* you are done—meet the interviewer's silence with some confident silence of your own. Then, break it with a question so that, once again, you can feel in control of the interview.

Don't worry, be positive

Go into the interview thinking, "I am going to get this job." You'll perform much better if you are confident (but not cocky).

Barry, a business associate of mine, switched jobs five times in the first 15 years of his career. He had very few interviews during those years, but he made the ones he did have really count.

One time, Barry got a call from an executive recruiter (or headhunter, as they are also commonly known) who wanted to tell him about a terrific new position. When the headhunter finished describing the job, Barry said, "Boy, that job has my name on it. What are they offering?"

The recruiter told Barry the top salary. It wasn't bad, but it was $10,000 less than Barry wanted if he were going to uproot himself again. "Well, Jane," he told the recruiter. "I wanted a lot more money than that."

"That's all I can squeeze out of them," said Jane. "That is the absolute top of the salary range for this position." Barry was not deterred. "Send me over there," he said. "Once they meet me, they'll come up with the extra dough."

After a great deal of hemming and hawing, Jane gave in. Barry, an experienced and confident interviewer, got the salary he wanted. (If you're wondering about how Barry negotiated this great salary package, you'll find the details in Chapter 13.)

Do you want that job?

If you want the job, go into the interview with the attitude that it's yours for the taking. Don't be cocky, but do be confident. Express your enthusiasm for the job and for the opportunity to be considered for it. And be positive about everything, even the weather.

Think of the type of people you would like to work with. They are happy to be on the job, bright, willing to help. Your goal is to convince the interviewer that he or she would like to work with *you*.

Do you know what they're writing about?

Not to make you more nervous, but if you're just graduating from college, you have something else to contend with—your generation has been getting a bad rap in the media. Countless articles in human resource journals and major consumer publications such as *Working Woman* and *Business Week* have characterized you and your peers as a hard-to-manage lot.

You're supposedly part of the "brash pack"—a group of spoiled brats who want the corner office and all the other perks of seniority without being ready to pay the dues everyone else has paid, without even wanting to take the time to learn to do your jobs right.

Sound as if you have a strike against you before you even apply for the job?

With some human resource departments and hiring managers, you do. The fact that you are faced with this disadvantage means that you must try even harder to convince the interviewer that you will be a trainable, hard-working employee—who will wait at least a year before requesting a corner office and a company Mercedes.

And that all those *other* entry-level candidates are the ones the magazines have been writing about!

Chapter 9

The top 75

Counting down the favorite
interview questions of all time

This is not exactly the most thrilling of hit parades, but it probably will be more useful to you than any *Rolling Stone* list of top hits.

Like television plots, all interview questions fall into roughly three groups:

1. Factual questions about your education and job experience.

2. Questions designed to determine who you really are and what you're made of.

3. Questions that will help the interviewer predict how you might perform on the job.

In the preceding chapters, I've discussed, in a general way, how you will answer these questions. This chapter will present a laundry list of questions. There will be a brief discussion about how you should frame your replies after groups of related questions.

You should not spend time preparing answers to all of these questions in advance, writing them down and memorizing them. If you did that, you might not go on your first interview until you were eligible for Medicare. But you should have the necessary facts to answer them in some relatively retrievable portion of your brain.

Questions about your education and job experience

1. What extracurricular activities were you active in? What made you choose those activities? Which of them did you most enjoy? Why?

2. Do you hold any leadership positions while you were in college? What do you think you learned?

3. What did you learn from (or, why don't I see any) internships on your resume? How did you get those internships? What was the most valuable thing you learned from each?

4. What were the most valuable lessons you learned from your part-time job?

5. If you were to start college over again tomorrow, what courses would you take? Why?

6. In what courses did you get your best grades? Why?

7. In what courses did you get your worst grades? Why? How do you think that will affect your performance on the job?

8. What were the factors that led you to select your college?

9. What led you to choose that major over others?

10. What type of student were you?

11. What sort of grades did you get? In your major? In your minor?

12. Which courses did you like the most? Why?

13. Which courses did you like the least? Why?

14. What are your most memorable experiences from college?

15. Why did you (or didn't you) decide to go to graduate school?

What the interviewer *really* wants to know

These questions might seem prosaic enough, but they all have a hidden agenda. The interviewer is really probing to determine how ambitious and how "trainable" you are.

No company really believes that someone is going to come out of college or graduate school and be productive immediately. Many are willing to invest in training to have people "forget what they learned in school and do things the *right* way," even if that takes months.

Therefore, the interviewer could very well be probing to see whether you're a know-it-all or sensible enough to know you still have a lot to learn.

The interviewer also is probing for the amount of ambition you have. He or she is also interested in determining the extent to which you have been pampered—or used to having things go your way with very little effort on your part.

Your First Interview

So, let's say you haven't run up a huge list of extracurricular accomplishments because you really had to hit the books to get good grades. If the interviewer asks, "Why didn't you get more involved in outside activities?" don't reply, "Oh, I spent a lot of time studying and I didn't want those things to get in the way of my social life."

Instead, say, "I got involved in a few things. I wish I had done more, but I really was interested in my studies. I cracked the books every night, and that's what enabled me to finish second in the class."

It is always a good idea to portray yourself as a well-rounded person. If your weren't a member of many official school clubs or teams, talk about other activities you engaged in during college. Did you tutor other students? Did you work to gain extra course credit?

A friend of mine had to work his way through college, holding down a number of menial positions totally unrelated to the career he hoped eventually to enter. He simply could not afford to be on low-paying internships during his summers or involve himself in a lot of extracurricular activities. He had to pump gas.

This presented a quandary during his interview at a publishing company, a very internship-oriented field.

My friend knew questions about these things would come up from his interviewer. Therefore, he was prepared with answers like, "I wish I'd had more time to do things like work on the school paper, but whenever I wasn't studying, I pretty much had to work to pay for college. During all of those jobs, though, I learned a number of things that people learn only after they've been in their careers for a while, like how to work with others and how to manage my time."

He turned a possible negative into a salient positive.

"Which courses did you like best?" Concentrate on the skills you developed in some of your courses—writing ability, debating skills, language skills—that will serve you well in this job. When naming your favorite courses or talking about your most memorable experiences, focus on those that are career-oriented, assuming you took courses related to the job at hand.

When asked about your least favorite courses, of course you will pick one *not* related to your eventual career. Try to develop answers that have to do with the *subject*, rather than such things as the professor's personality or the workload.

When answering questions 3 and 4, about your internship or part-time work, stress how the real-world experience complemented the academic training you received.

Question 5 asks what you would do if you were to start college over. Think about changes you would have made in your course selection that would have produced a better candidate for *the job you're interviewing for*. Should you have taken more marketing courses, an accounting course, a statistics seminar?

Now, about your grades. Many companies will ask to see copies of college transcripts, so you may as well come clean now. If you flunked every accounting course and have even a modicum of intelligence, you're probably not applying for an accounting job, right? Hopefully you can blame the bad grades you might have received in some of your electives on the amount of time and effort you were putting into your major.

When discussing your major, it's a good idea to be decisive, to say that you are convinced you chose the right field, even though it might have taken you a while to find it. "I'm really glad I majored in Pseudoscience. I only wish that I had known a little more about it when I began my studies. I could have taken a couple of other courses in the discipline as an undergraduate."

Why didn't you enroll in graduate school? You were chomping at the bit to get out into the real world, to start working at a company like this one. Graduate degrees are not necessary for every profession, of course. But even if you are planning to earn your M.B.A. some time in the future, there's nothing at all wrong with wanting to have some work experience to apply to your studies.

Questions about who you are
(and what you're made of)

16. Please tell me a little bit about yourself.

17. What do you consider your key strengths?

18. What do you consider your key weaknesses? What do you think you will do about them?

19. Have you ever had a weakness in the past that you've been able to overcome? How did you accomplish this?

20. Do you think that you'll prefer to work with others or by yourself? Are there experiences you have had in school or in part-time jobs that support that?

21. What do you want to accomplish in your life?

22. Do you have any plans to further your education?

23. During your internships (or part-time jobs), what sort of evaluations did you get from supervisors?

24. What supervisor did you like the best? Why did you like him or her?

25. What supervisor did you like the least? What did you not like about him or her?

26. Looking back on the experience, do you think you could have done anything differently to get along with the supervisor a little better?

27. What are some of the things you do in your spare time? What are your favorite hobbies? Do you play any sports?

28. How do you handle yourself when you're having a conflict with someone? Are you confrontational? Do you avoid that person? Why? How do you think you'll behave when you have a problem with a co-worker?

29. If you could change one thing about your personality with a snap of your fingers, what would it be? Why?

30. If I met some of your peers from college, what do you think they would say about you?

31. Would you describe yourself as a risk-taker or someone who plays it safe?

32. Why should I consider you a strong applicant for this position?

Tough, aren't they?

If you're hit with a series of questions from the previous list, you'll feel like you've been put through the wringer.

Only the most annoying people *don't* find it difficult to talk about themselves in a flattering way. And that's what you'll be doing on the interview—constantly blowing your own horn until even you will want to change the tune.

You'll be saying what a great guy your friends think you are, what a pleasure your supervisors thought it was to have you on their team, that there are only a few little adjustments you'd like to make to your personality. Why, this can all sound pretty sickening.

But don't get carried away with yourself. When you're answering these questions:

- Remember that companies are looking for these traits: enthusiasm, confidence, energy, dependability, honesty and pride in work.

- Formulate your answers so that they suggest these characteristics. Think about what you would want in an ideal employee if *you* owned a company. You'd want problem-solvers, team players, people willing to work hard, people who enjoy what they're doing, wouldn't you? So do the interviewers you'll be meeting.

- Remember not to volunteer any negative information about yourself unless you are specifically asked for it. When you *are* asked for it, try to turn it into a positive.

For example, "Well, I have had a problem with procrastination, but I have really solved it. What I learned in college was to work on the tasks I least like first, and then the rest of my assignments seemed easy."

- Let the interviewer know that you have no problem getting along with other people. However, every job situation forces us to get along with people we might not choose to socialize with. Acknowledge this and talk about how you've managed to get along with a wide variety of other people.

- On questions about self-improvement and future plans, remember that you must exhibit loyalty. Don't say that you can't wait to get to graduate school to better yourself or you hope to be in your own business in five years. Formulate answers that show you want to be in a better position *at their company* and that you're willing to accommodate their needs—rather than yours—first.

Questions that help the interviewer predict how you'll perform on the job

More and more employers are using "situational questions" in hopes of better predicting employee behavior on the job. These can go something like this:

33. In your internships and part-time positions, what types of supervisors got the most out of you? Why?

34. What college professors did you most enjoy? Why?

35. What most influenced you to choose the career you're ready to begin?

36. When you're faced with a particularly tough decision, how do you go about making it? Can you give me an example from your college days?

37. The successful candidate for this position will be working with some highly trained individuals who have been with us for a long time. If you get the job, how will you make sure that you fit in?

38. What are you looking for in a job?

39. Let's say your supervisor gave you an assignment that you didn't understand and then left town for a week. Assume he or she is unreachable. What would you do?

40. Have your hobbies or sports activities taught you any lessons that you'd bring to the job?

41. Describe your ideal boss.

42. This is a large (or a small) company. Do you think you'd like that sort of environment? Why? What do you think you might not like about it?

43. What do you know about the financial aspects of this business? Have any of your studies or readings helped you know about how we budget? What affects our bottom line?

44. Are you an organized person?

45. Do you manage your time well?

46. If your supervisor told you to do something a certain way, and you knew that way was dead wrong, what would you do?

47. You won't be managing people for a while, but if you were, how do you think your subordinates describe you?

48. After you're on the job for a while, how do you think your co-workers would describe you?

49. Why are you interested in this position?

50. How long do you think this position will be challenging to you? What do you think you would like to do next?

51. Why this company? What about it appeals to you most?

52. Is there anything about this company or job that makes you apprehensive? Why?

53. What aspects of this job do you think you'll find the most interesting?

54. What aspects do you think you'll find the least interesting?

55. How will you react to doing the least interesting or least pleasant parts of this job?

56. How do you think this job will help you achieve your long-term career objectives?

57. Describe your ideal job based on what you know of your discipline and this industry right now.

58. How do you think the job you're applying for matches up with that description?

59. Are there any glaring shortcomings to the position based on your description of the ideal job?

60. Were there any unusual difficulties you had to overcome to do so well in college? How did you do it?

61. What did you spend most of your time doing during your internship(s)?

62. Are you able to work overtime? On weekends?

63. Your lack of experience bothers me. Why do *you* think I should I hire someone just out of school, like you?

64. What do you want most out of your job? Money? Satisfaction? Power?

65. Can you perform well under pressure? How do you know that?

66. What does the word "success" mean to you? How about "failure"?

What they're trying this time

All of these questions are designed to determine whether you have "organizational fit." The interviewer wants to know if you'll stick around for a while to become a valued employee, or whether the organization and/or you will soon wish you'd never heard of each other.

If you're a recent college graduate, you'll be at a distinct disadvantage in answering many of these questions. So:

- Admit when you don't have all of the answers. Or begin a lot of your answers with "I think..." or "From what I know about the company..."

- Remember the attributes the company wants most in its employees and display them every chance you get.

- Don't sound squeamish about going through the school of hard knocks. As I've mentioned, many baby boomers think that baby busters (you) have a severe "attitude problem." Tell the interviewer, "Sure, I know this position has its share of unpleasant duties, but I'm sure everyone who's had this position has learned a lot by doing them."

- Be positive about your negatives.

- Don't be afraid to tell the interviewer that you'll ask for help in certain situations. Not many companies are looking for 22-year-old know-it-alls.

- Go in prepared with this winning answer about your ideal supervisor:

  "The ideal supervisor has a great deal of experience in the field and enjoys sharing it. I think he or she should delegate the challenging tasks of the department to the most deserving employees."

  "(Management expert) Peter Drucker has said that 'the manager's role is to give employees the tools they need to get the job done.' I think that's a good description of the ideal supervisor—someone who provides the resources and, when necessary, the knowledge employees need to do and enjoy their jobs."

- If you don't really know where you want to be five or more years down the road (and how many of us really do?), say so, but in a positive way. Your answer should be something like:

  "Well, I loved studying biochemistry and that's why I want to work at a leading company in the field, like yours. I hope that I can learn a great deal more about the field, and that I excel enough to be given additional challenges here. I'm only sure right now that I want to work and do well in this discipline."

- Dazzle 'em with footwork. Show off the research you've done on the company. Embellish your answers to these questions with facts you've learned about the company and the industry.

Wrapping up

Just when you thought the grilling was over, the interviewer could very well have a crop of seemingly innocuous questions. Take them seriously.

67. Is there anything else I should know about you?

68. Would you be willing to relocate?

69. Have you been interviewing for other positions?

70. Have you received any offers?

71. When do you have to hear from us? What is your availability?

72. What do you think of our compensation package?

73. How does this position seem to compare to others for which you've interviewed?

74. May I contact your references?

You might not think you have anything else left to tell the interviewer, but you'd better have! Here's someone giving you a chance to *close the sale.*

Develop a short answer to question 67, one that plays upon your strengths, accomplishments, skills and areas of knowledge. For instance, "Mr. Brown, I think we've covered everything, but I want to reemphasize the key strengths that I would bring to this position."

If you are interested in the position, don't be cute. Say that you are available immediately, or as soon as you can relocate—whatever is convenient for you and the employer. And tell the truth about other positions. You needn't bring up the names of the employers. Make it clear that the position for which you are interviewing is the one you're most interested in.

I also would advise against talking about salary at this stage. Get a sense of what the package (compensation and benefits) is, but wait until you get an offer to negotiate. That is the time when you have the most leverage.

If you're asked for references, tell the interviewer you will back to him or her with a list of references that afternoon or, if it is already late in the day, the next morning. Be sure to notify your prospective references that a call might be coming from Mr. Brown at XYZ Company.

If your references are indeed going to say wonderful things about you, they should be prepared to do so.

75. Do you have any questions?

This is the surefire sign that the interview is drawing to a close, and if you haven't asked a question until now, it's also probably a surefire bet that you're not getting the job.

You should be asking plenty of questions throughout the interview. If, at this point, you have all the information you need to make an informed decision, be decisive and say so.

If reading this list makes you feel as if you've run the gauntlet, remember you'll feel much worse after your interview if you fail to prepare to answer such most-asked questions.

Chapter 10

"What did you say?"

Know your rights as
an interviewee

In an ideal world, companies and managers would judge their employees only on the basis of their job performance, and candidates would be measured only against a set of criteria deemed important for doing the job well.

Our world isn't ideal. In the *real* world, few people can judge others with pure objectivity. As a result, many managers and even entire companies and professions discriminate.

The most unpleasant manifestations of the real world for too many job candidates are questions and remarks related to sex, race, ethnic background, marital status and all of the other ridiculous traits upon which the ignorant and sometimes not so ignorant think it fair to judge people.

What can you do if you come face to face with racism, sexism or some other ugly "ism" during a job interview?

All too many candidates feel that they have to endure and answer politely every question an interviewer asks, no matter how distasteful or irrelevant.

That's pure nonsense. Candidates have rights. If the interviewer doesn't seem to know what these rights are, *you* should.

Your First Interview

This chapter will explain your rights as an interviewee and what you can do if you feel an interviewer has acted inappropriately or unlawfully.

What does *that* have to do with my job?

It's pretty easy to tell when a question is inappropriate—it has little or nothing to do with how the candidate might perform on the job. And that's pretty much what the law states—interviewers can ask questions that have to do with job performance. When they ask questions that are unrelated to the work to be performed, they could be skating on thin ice.

Every state has fair-employment-practices laws governing the screening of job candidates and lists of questions considered unlawful for employers to ask on job applications and during interviews. Check with your state's Fair Employment Practices Commission for more details.

In the meantime, I can give you the following general guidelines that may help you recognize discriminatory or otherwise illegal interview and job application questions:

- **Name.** Sure, that seems innocent enough. Prospective employers will need to know your name to address you. But in many states, you are protected from questions that seek to determine your birth name if you've had it legally changed, or your maiden name if you're a married woman. However, employers *are* permitted to ask what other names they should check to determine your employment history.

- **Marital/family status.** Employers are not permitted to ask about your marital status or plans for marriage. Likewise, they are forbidden from asking women about their plans for having children.

  I think this is an area in which it is very easy for women especially to "open the door" to a host of questions you aren't required to answer—unless you bring them up. After all, what could seem more innocent than chit-chatting about your fiancé or spouse or kids? Do you really want to discuss your tentative plans for having a child within a year? Think about it.

- **Age.** Employers cannot ask for your birth date or about facts that might reveal your birth date, such as the year you graduated from high school.

- **Creed.** Under no circumstances is an employer permitted to ask about your religious affiliation or the religious holidays you observe. In addition, interviewers are not permitted to make even simple statements such as, "This is a Christian (or Jewish or Muslim) company," perhaps looking for some sort of reaction from you as a prospective employee.

- **Nationality.** Employers are generally forbidden to ask about your ancestry, descent, parentage or nationality, that of your parents or spouse, or inquire about your "mother tongue." Technically speaking, an interviewer could not ask, "Is that an Irish name?" but he or she *could* ask you what language(s) you are proficient in. However, because of new, tougher immigration laws, companies are permitted to have you produce proof of citizenship or status as a resident, such as a "green card."

- **Race.** Employers cannot ask you about the color of your skin or that of your relatives or spouse.

- **Military service.** The employer can ask how long and in what branch of the service you were in, but not the type of discharge you received.

- **Physical condition.** The 1992 Americans with Disabilities Act (ADA) precludes employers from asking about diseases for which you've been treated, whether you've ever been hospitalized, if you've ever filed for worker's compensation and if you are taking any medication.

  Also, while they cannot ask something like, "Do you have any physical disabilities?" they certainly can ask, "Are you able to perform the job for which your are applying either with or without an accommodation?"

- **Photograph.** Employers are not permitted to ask for photographs to be attached to job applications.

- **Organizations.** Employers can ask about your membership in organizations that *you* consider important to the performance of the job. Otherwise, this can be another sneaky way to find out about religion (if you're a member of B'nai B'rith or the Christian Church Fellowship, for example), race (if you're a member of the NAACP and it's not obvious you are African American), political affiliation, etc.

How to react when you're asked a "wrong" question

Despite a plethora of lawsuits charging employers with discriminatory hiring practices, unlawful questions still are commonly asked during interviews. This is particularly true of interviews by hiring managers, who generally have not received the extensive education on legal issues human resource professionals now routinely undergo.

What do you do if you're asked a question that you believe to be unlawful?

You have three choices:

1. You can refuse, on principle, to answer any unlawful question, even if you'd come up smelling like a rose anyway.

2. You can be a pragmatist and provide any answers you feel wouldn't hurt you, while you tactfully sidestep illegal questions you think could hurt you.

3. You can use a mixture of both approaches.

Let's say you have an "obviously" Italian last name, like Rutigliano. You greet the interviewer and he says, "Boy, that's Italian, isn't it?" You should smile politely and not answer at all. It's quite possible he meant absolutely no offense. However, if later the interviewer pursues the line of questioning with, "Were your parents born in the United States or on the other side?" you can dodge it one more time by saying something like, "They don't remember. They were just little babies." But by now you should be wary for any further signs of prejudice or insensitivity.

If the interviewer still doesn't get the hint, and continues to allude to your heritage, then you should point out to him that he is doing something illegal. You might say, "I really don't see what my ancestry has to do with my application for this job. You must know that you're not supposed to ask me questions like this."

Believe it or not, you could still stay on the interviewer's good side if you handle the situation in a diplomatic way. At the same time, you will have put him on notice that you are aware of the law and do not take it as lightly as he obviously does. You also have told him that he has opened himself up to a discrimination charge.

Such a line of questioning, however, might well indicate that you don't want to work for this supervisor under any circumstances. He's obviously an ignorant, insensitive person.

Harassment: A problem that won't go away

Talk to any employment lawyer and he or she will tell you that sexual discrimination cases are the largest part of their practices. Since the Clarence Thomas nomination hearings, sexual harassment has received a lot of attention in the business and general-interest press. As more multimillion-dollar settlements are being won against companies that allow sexual harassment to continue, more and more employers are beginning to see the issue as a potential powder keg—and ordering up training programs to discourage it.

Despite all of this, however, sexual harassment still exists in the workplace—and the interviewing office.

Women have told us about being asked to dinner during interviews with male hiring managers. Others talked about interviewers staring at their chests throughout the interview.

What are you to do if this happens? Well, unfortunately, the best choice is to do nothing—bring the interview to a close as quickly as possible and scratch the position off your list. Then, you should follow up with the human resources department and report the interviewer's behavior.

If you still want to work at that company, ask about positions in other departments. If you encounter this kind of discrimination in your interview with the human resources department, scratch the company off your list altogether. You would undoubtedly be walking into a work situation that is very uncomfortable.

Married with children?

Even when sex is not the issue, *your* sex still might be. Some employers still have the nerve to ask women about their marital or familial status. Many supervisors don't want to offer a position to a woman who they think is going to get pregnant and leave them in a few months.

Your best bet is to meet such questions head on. Your marital status and family plans are simply none of your prospective employer's business. Make this a non-issue by talking about such things as your excellent attendance record and the need you see for a healthy balance in your life.

Your First Interview

If the interviewer pursues this line of questioning, remind him that your husband (or lack of one) and family (or lack of one) are not what you came to his office to discuss—that you are interested in committing yourself to the job he or she has open or you wouldn't have shown up for the interview.

Remember, too, that many interviewers are aware of the laws surrounding questions about sex, sexual orientation and family status. However, all bets are off when the interviewee introduces the material into the interview situation.

For instance, a female acquaintance of mine, Karen, interviewed at one of the largest companies in the country. The skilled interviewer kept shifting gears between very job-related and very personal questions.

Although Karen was a savvy interviewee and had little trouble deflecting the questions she knew to be inappropriate, she let her guard down once, beginning an answer with "My husband."

The interviewer pounced on that as quickly as a salesman can get his foot in an open door. She began asking questions about what Karen's husband did and how he "felt about his wife having a job that required a lot of travel."

The interviewer apparently wanted to know what Karen's career and family plans were, but knew better than to come right out and ask such unlawful questions.

Once *Karen* introduced the subject of her husband, however, the interviewer felt her family life was fair game. She couldn't ask anything as obviously unlawful as, "Are you married?" or "Don't you want to have children, and won't your career interfere with that?" But she still wanted to know the answers to those questions.

I must reiterate that you should never bring up personal material yourself unless you're willing to answer questions about it. Savvy interviewers will grab at any opportunity to get information they want without running the risk of ending up in court. Their defense will be, "*I* never asked about her family. *She* brought it up." And while it still might not be entirely on the "up and up," it may well prove enough of a defense.

They are usually much more subtle

However, many employers or supervisors who discriminate will try to elicit information they consider damaging in subtle ways.

For instance, an interviewer might ask someone he or she suspects of being an immigrant if English is spoken at home.

Here's an example of a very subtle form of discrimination. A friend of mine applied for a job at one of the big tobacco companies. She went through three interviews, and the company was obviously very high on her. During her last interview, she was asked if she would like a cigarette. She said, "No thanks. I don't smoke." That was the last she heard from them.

Notice, the interviewer never asked, "Are you a smoker?" or "Do you smoke?" Turning down an applicant because she refused to engage in an unhealthy activity might put the company on questionable legal and public relations ground.

But the information was gotten nevertheless, and the hiring decision was made based on that illicit information.

(When I heard the story, I couldn't help but wish she had answered, "No thanks. I don't smoke *during interviews.*" Perfectly true, and nearly as coy as their gambit!)

What to do after the fact

If you are not offered a position after being asked unlawful questions, you might have grounds for charging the employer with discrimination. The interviewer asked non-job-related questions, and you have reason to believe that your refusal to answer these questions or the answers you provided led to your not being hired.

The operative word here is "might." You would have to prove that the questions were asked for the purpose of discriminating among applicants for an illegal reason.

For instance, if the manager asking all those questions about Italian ancestry subsequently hired another Italian, you wouldn't have much of a claim, despite the fact that you were asked illegal questions.

If you *do* think that you have grounds for a charge of discrimination, you should file your charges simultaneously with the appropriate state agency and the Equal Employment Opportunity Commission (EEOC). The EEOC generally will wait until the state agency has conducted an investigation, then conduct an investigation of its own.

As you would expect when dealing with government agencies, you might not hear anything for years. When the EEOC does act, it may be solely to determine whether there is reason to believe your charge is true. Therefore, if you are anxious for justice, you should request that the EEOC issue you a notice to sue 180 days after you file your charge.

If you are right

If the EEOC determines in your favor, it will attempt to mediate the dispute between you and the employer. Failing to arrange for such an agreement, the Commission will either file a suit or issue you a letter giving you the right to sue the employer. You must file your suit within 90 days of receiving such a letter.

Even if you go through all this trouble and win your lawsuit, don't expect to receive a colossal settlement. The most you'll probably get from the employer for an interview "indiscretion" is the equivalent of about one year's salary.

As I've stressed throughout this book, the primary thing to remember about interviews is that you are there as a participant, not as a powerless victim.

If you feel that the interviewer is asking you questions that shouldn't be asked, the first step is to try to shrug them off and change the direction of the conversation.

The next step is to inform the employer that you know he or she is doing something unlawful. This should put any interviewer on warning that you won't submit to illegal interview behavior, or the discrimination that might result from it, without a fight.

The last step is to terminate the interview and, possibly, seek to bring formal charges against the company and the interviewer.

Chapter 11

"It ain't over 'til it's over"

The fine art of following up

Yogi Berra said many memorable things, most of them head-scratchers, but none as famous as the line, "It ain't over 'til it's over." If the interview is to prove meaningful for you, and you want to increase your chances of landing that job—even if you're utterly sure that you knocked the interviewer's socks off—the interview is *not* over when you leave your would-be employer's office.

To increase your chances of landing that job, you must take several follow-up steps.

Don't be just another candidate

I hope you'll learn at least one great lesson from every boss you'll have during your career. One of my most memorable bosses taught me several lessons that I find myself applying at least once every week.

The single most valuable lesson he taught me was that the world was full of mediocre people. It is, therefore, relatively easy (he asserted) to be perceived as excellent—so easy that it makes no sense *not* to take steps to rise above the crowd.

The important thing to remember is to *act promptly*. When you meet someone who might be important to you (such as your interviewer), write him or her a letter and see that it's mailed that very day. Think how great you'll look next to others who said that they'd contact that person and never did—or did so *weeks* later.

Take my word for it, that's great advice. On the day of your interview, use it. Do not pass "Go." Proceed directly to your word processor, type a letter to the person who interviewed you and walk it to the mail box.

The letter should express your gratitude for the chance to be considered for the position. It should, like the initial cover letter you sent, emphasize one of your key strengths. It should also mention something you or the interviewer said.

Most importantly, the follow-up letter should let the "real you" show through. After all, you are now writing to someone you've met and who, presumably, has gotten to know you pretty well. There's a good example of a follow-up letter on page 163.

Robert N. Johnsmeyer
725 Crescent Avenue
Manhattan Beach, CA 98765
213-555-3434

April 1, 1996

Mr. John Edelstein
Vice President/Distribution
ABD Neckwear
11200 Stemmons
Boston, MA 02222

Dear Mr. Edelstein:

It certainly was a pleasure meeting with you today and learning more about the entry-level dispatching position at ABD Neckwear. Thank you once again for your time and for the information you shared with me.

I feel confident that my education in cartography will be invaluable in helping the company achieve the most efficient use of its fleet. Your department's achievements in distribution are extraordinary, and I'm sure I would find the environment stimulating and challenging. I was especially interested in your description of the employee suggestion system that has helped the company realize important savings.

Mr. Edelstein, I found our time together today not only informative, but enjoyable. I am sure that we would greatly enjoy working together.

I look forward to hearing from you in the very near future.

Sincerely yours,

Robert N. Johnsmeyer

Robert N. Johnsmeyer

Giving references

If the interviewer asks for a list of references, tell him or her you will get back with a list that afternoon or, if it the interview ends late in the day, the following morning.

Does this make you seem unprepared? Shouldn't you go into the interview with the list? After all, your resume says, "References available upon request," and here's the request.

Well, in the world of interviews, stalling for a little time before giving the references is SOP (standard operating procedure).

The reason you want to wait is that you'll want to forewarn your prospective references that a call might be coming from Mr. Somebody of ABC Corporation. If they are going to give you a good reference, they should be prepared. And if they're not, you'll want to change the list—fast.

How do you know what they'll say?

You've worked too hard to get this job to let a reference check blow it for you. That means you should manage that process as well as you've managed every other part of the interview.

The first step is to line up your references before going on your first interview. You should speak to all of the people you'll be including on your list and let each one know how you will be presenting yourself and what exactly you'll be saying about your affiliation with him or her.

It's a good idea to follow up these conversations with a letter and a copy of your resume. This will allow your reference to see just how you're presenting your job, internship or independent course work. Your resume will also tell him or her what you are saying about your abilities and accomplishments.

Unsure about what one of these references might say about you? Ask. If you feel that he or she remembers your relationship differently than you do, resolve the situation.

Don't expect your interviewer to fill in the blanks

In these litigious times, many references are afraid to say anything about a past associate for fear of being sued for libel or slander. Therefore, you should be aware of the things that your references *won't* say.

If you know that a reference will give only the bare facts of date of employment and job title, try your best to leave him or her off the list. Employers might read unwillingness to say anything as merely avoidance of saying anything bad.

Softening the blow

But no matter how careful you are at this stage of the process, there's a chance that the manager or professor with an unfavorable opinion of you will be contacted. If you think this might damage your chances of securing the job you covet, do your best to score a preemptive strike.

Tell the hiring manager or personnel department why you might receive an unfavorable reference from that manager. One of the most common and easily accepted reasons for a bad reference is the vague "personality conflict." Indicate that you and the manager did not get along, but that there are other people at the organization who can vouch for the quality of your work. Give one or more of their names.

Once again, follow up

It's a good idea to follow up with your references to see if they were called and, if they were, how the questioning went. What were some of the things that your prospective employer wanted to know? Is it obvious from their questions that one particular area of your background is troubling them?

If that's the case, you might be able to overcome their objections with a follow-up phone call a week to 10 days after the interview.

It's perfectly acceptable for you to inquire about the status of the position. Have they filled it? Do they expect to reach a decision in the near future? When? Are you still in the running?

This phone call will give the interviewer an opportunity to ask you about anything he or she has heard during the reference check that causes concern.

What if you change your mind?

Did something during the interview make you decide that you didn't want to work at the company? Then politely take yourself out of the running. Write a letter to the screening interviewer and the hiring manager indicating that you thank them for the opportunity to interview, but have decided to pursue other options.

Following up in a professional manner will leave your interviewers with a positive impression, so they will be less likely to label you "unreliable," "indecisive" or worse. You never know: Someday you might decide that company is perfect for you.

No job is over until
the paperwork is done

Remember: Write a thank-you letter on the day of your interview, follow up with your references and respond immediately to the interviewer's requests for more information.

Your prompt attention to these matters is sure to help you stand out from the crowd of candidates. And it will serve as just one more indication of what a terrific, timely employee you will be.

Chapter 12

A learning experience

Putting together everything you learned during the interview

The interview is a two-way street. It is an opportunity for the employer to learn about you and vice versa. You should learn as much as you can about the employer, not only by asking some of the questions discussed in Chapter 9, but by observing the offices, the attitudes of interviewers and other people you come into contact with, as well as any nuances in the way your interviews were conducted.

Seemed like a good idea at the time

My friend Tony is a crackerjack writer and editor. His work brought him into fairly frequent contact with Bill, a public relations executive for a large consulting firm.

Tony was struggling and not making much money, so his antennae went up when Bill moved on to another consulting outfit as head of public relations. Bill's job would be to build a complete public relations staff and program from scratch. Tony, having heard all about Bill's house in an expensive suburb, his family's annual trips to Europe and his new Mercedes, wanted to know just when Bill would be hiring staff at QRS Consulting.

Tony didn't have to wait too long. Bill not only told him about the number-two position in P.R., but informed him he was a "shoe-in" for the lucrative job. However, Tony would have to meet with the director of human resources and the vice president of communications before he was officially hired.

Bill seemed very happy in his new job, so Tony was initially excited about the interviews.

When they were over, however, Tony decided he wouldn't take the job if it paid twice as much.

What happened during the interviews?

Well, Tony picked up so many "negative vibes" during his screening that he knew he would absolutely loathe QRS. For instance, in his interview with Mr. Ego, the director of human resources, he was asked almost no questions. Ego talked about what an exciting place QRS was and how hard everyone worked. His favorite phrases were "kicking butt and taking down names" and "show 'em no mercy." He used "I" and "me" an insufferable number of times. Through it all, he acted like he couldn't have cared less about what Tony had to say about his own potential contributions.

The vice president of communications was even worse. He talked on and on about how hard everyone at QRS worked, how many nights *he* had to work "all kinds of hours," and how arbitrary the many last-minute changes made by the company president often were.

At the end of the ordeal, Bill took Tony for a bite to eat in the company cafeteria. Tony noticed people practically running down the food line, wolfing down their sandwiches while they read work-related materials, then rushing back to their offices. It was the quietest cafeteria he'd ever seen.

Tony's spirits were somewhere below the linoleum, but Bill was still giving the company, his department and his job high marks. He loved it.

Ego called Tony to offer him the job next day. Tony said he'd have to think it over and Ego acted as if Tony had rocks in his head. "What could there be to think about?" Ego blustered. "We're offering you a lot of money, and we'll be as big as IBM some day."

Tony called Bill the next day to say that he wouldn't be joining QRS. Bill was dumbfounded when Tony gave his reasons: "Neither Ego nor your boss asked me a single question about me or my qualifications. All they did was talk about how hard they worked. QRS is strictly for Type A personalities. The company couldn't care less about its employees as long as they stay late."

Bill put up a mild argument and told Tony that he had gotten the wrong impression. Tony told Bill not to expect him to change his mind this sunspot cycle.

Bill, citing the hours and the poor way his department was treated, quit QRS less than six months later.

Take stock

This is only a slight exaggeration of a true story, but I think it demonstrates that you should use the interview as an opportunity to soak up impressions about the company like a sponge. Does it seem like a good place to work? Is your boss going to be friend or foe? Are your colleagues going to work with you and support you or quietly trace targets on your back?

Right after you get home from the interview, write and mail your thank-you letters, and contact the people you've given as references, take a moment or two to sit down in a quiet room with a pen and paper and write down all of your impressions about the company and the people you met. Don't worry about being grammatically correct or especially descriptive. Just record all of your impressions, both good and bad. Here are some questions that might help you during this process:

- What were your impressions of the people you came into contact with, other than the interviewers? Did they seem happy to be at work, or did the place feel like a funeral parlor—at midnight? Were people open, relaxed and friendly, or uptight, rushed and brusque? (If you could practically see employees' nerve endings, you probably should look for a job somewhere else.)

- Did the interviewers seem genuinely interested in you or only in your qualifications? Were you treated like an individual or a commodity?

- Did your prospective boss seem like a workaholic? Was his or her desk teeming with papers? Did he or she talk about long hours and all of the details he or she had to oversee? Did he or she mention other members of his staff at all?

My advice is to avoid working for the work-obsessed. You can never do enough for them; they will never give you a lot of responsibility, and they probably will be stingy with compliments and credit for your accomplishments.

Workaholics are insecure people convinced that no one can do the job as well as they can. No matter how terrific you are, you won't convince a workaholic boss to give you the running room you need or want.

- What does your instinct tell you? There's something to be said for "going with your gut." Do you think you'd get along with the interviewer if he or she was your boss? Would he or she be overly critical or helpful and supportive?

- How did the interviewers react to your questions? Did they seem to welcome the opportunity to give you information, or were they reticent to share details or, worse yet, annoyed with you for putting *them* to the test?

  If the latter was the case, think long and hard about how these people are likely to act *after* you take the job. They'll probably display even less patience and willingness to share.

- What did your prospective boss's eyes tell you? Did he or she engage in a staring contest, study you for clues to your emotions, overly enjoy the role of the Grand Inquisitor? Or was he or she direct, while still seeming friendly, open, honest and caring?

Keep your eyes peeled

Usually a company will convey a great deal about itself on its bulletin boards, in its reception area and along its main corridors. Did you see employee awards posted prominently, or does the company seem to give little recognition to the accomplishments of its employees? Are aphorisms posted here and there? Do they say something like, "If *you* aren't proud of it, don't ship it"? Or are they more like something you'd see in a government institution: "Radio-playing is grounds for termination"?

Look for all of the telltale clues that you can. Think about them and write down your impressions. If you are offered a job with the company, you will be faced with one of the biggest decisions of your life. Make sure you're appropriately armed with *all* of the information you need to make the right one.

Chapter 13

Negotiating your first salary

You want to be *paid* for working here?

There are many schools of thought when it comes to the question of how to handle the discussion of salary during job interviews. Some experts advise bringing the topic to a head as soon as possible after the preliminary part of the interview. Others suggest avoiding the subject entirely, as if getting a paycheck were some unspeakable practice.

Common sense dictates a course somewhere between these two extremes. I recommend that you avoid bringing up the subject of salary yourself during your screening and selection interviews. If the interviewer brings it up, answer his or her questions. But it's really in your best interest to avoid getting down to the brass tacks of salary negotiation until an offer has been made.

When we issued the first edition of this book in 1991, we were in the midst of a seller's market. Management gurus were speaking about the baby bust and the upward effects that a predicted dearth of qualified applicants would have on starting salaries. Now, we are in the midst of a "job bust," when many graduates are going a-begging for positions and salary increases are modest.

Therefore, in this chapter I now urge greater flexibility on your behalf when it comes to salary negotiations.

A buy-sell situation

The interview is a classic buy-sell situation. You are trying to sell yourself to a company and get the best price you can. The company is making sure that it wants to buy what you're offering, and, naturally, hopes to pay as little as you'll accept.

Not talking about price in a situation like this is ludicrous. But talking about it at the wrong time is foolish.

This brings to mind the example of Barry, whose story we read in Chapter 8. When he was told about the position he eventually secured, the executive recruiter told him that the job was paying a top salary of $80,000. Barry was seeking $90,000. Barry—who, of course, was much more experienced at job hunting than you are right now—firmly told the recruiter, "I want that job. Send me on the interview. After they've met me, they'll be willing to pay me what I want."

It sounds cocky, but Barry was absolutely right. He studiously avoided the subject of salary during the entire interview. When the interviewer finally asked, "What would it take to get you over here?" Barry said, "I understand the job has a top salary of $80,000." He waited for the interviewer to nod, then said, "Well, I would need more than that. I came here because the job sounded terrific. In fact, the job description Helen (the recruiter) gave me had my name written all over it." Eventually the employer came around to meet his demand. But only because Barry had already sold himself.

Timing is everything in life

This example should point out the biggest truism about salary discussion:

> You have nothing to gain by discussing dollars and cents before you've convinced the employer that you're the right person for the job. In other words, the best time to discuss salary is *after you get the offer.*

Most likely you won't find yourself in a situation similar to Barry's. Just getting out of college, you'll be applying for entry-level positions that have relatively narrow salary ranges. What's more, you don't really have that much to sell yet, and the competition is more fierce than it has been in decades.

Nevertheless, you are not a commodity. If you can stand apart from the crowd of applicants, if you can convince the employer that an extra couple of thousand dollars would be well-spent on a dynamo like you, then one of the only sure ways *not* to get it is by putting a price tag around your neck too early in the proceedings.

In Chapter 8, I stressed that showing an interest in the interviewer is critically important. Trying to speak about something—salary—that he or she has no *desire* to speak about until he finishes asking questions is one sure way to make the interviewer feel that you are self-absorbed and uninterested in anything but money.

Would you buy something from a salesperson who only wanted to impress upon you how much something cost?

Of course not.

Why would a company hire someone only interested in seeing how much he or she could get?

I, and most experienced hiring managers I know, have at least one story about candidates who ask only about salary, benefits and days off. None of these subjects is a good one to ask about when the employer first asks you if you have any questions!

What if the interviewer brings it up first?

You can always tell when an interviewer is paying people too little. This kind of interviewer will bring up salary early on to determine whether he or she can afford you before spending the time to interview you.

Okay, that might not always be the reason that the subject of salary is broached too early. It might just be that the interviewer is inexperienced or has a premonition that you'll want more than he or she can afford to pay.

Whatever the reason, if the subject of salary *does* come up too early, sidestep it. Remember: It can't possibly do you any good to discuss salary before you've sold the employer. So, handle the question as you would some of the sensitive questions we discussed at the beginning of Chapter 10—diplomatically avoid them. One of the following replies might prove useful:

- *"I have an idea of the salary range for the position from your ad (or from what the recruiter said). It sounds like a reasonable range to me."*

- *"I'm willing to consider any reasonable salary offer."*

- *"I'd like to hear a little more about what my responsibilities will be before I can feel comfortable about talking about a starting salary."*

- *"From what I know about the position and the company, I don't think we'll have any trouble agreeing on a fair salary."*

- *"I'm well aware of what starting salaries are for this position within the industry. I'm sure that if salaries here are comparable, we'll have no trouble coming to an agreement."*

Remember, you *don't* want to talk about money even though the employer brought it up. Defer, defer, defer the discussion until later.

Fielding the offer

So, you're an ace candidate. You have impressed the interviewer so much so that a couple of days later you get an offer by phone.

You're delirious. You want to shout with joy. After all, you've sold a stranger on yourself—that's a terrific vote of confidence. You got the job!

Don't get too carried away just yet. You've captured the high ground in your search for a job. Now you want to take advantage of that.

Earlier in the chapter, I stressed that the interview is a buy-sell situation. Now that the company is sold on you, *you're* the one who must make the decision to buy.

Take your time. You should never—repeat, *never*—accept a job the minute it's offered to you. Even though you've probably thought about little else since your last interview with the employer, and have thoroughly made up your mind that you will accept the job if it's offered, tell the company that you "need some time to consider it."

You could say you want to sleep on it, or think about it over the weekend, or talk it over with your spouse or "adviser."

Most companies will push you for a fairly quick response. The company has probably interviewed other promising candidates for the position and doesn't want to lose them if their leading candidate turns them down.

However, don't act before *you're* ready to. Tell the person making the offer that you need a short time to think it over, thank him or her profusely for thinking so highly of you and agree on a day and a time that you'll call back with your answer.

This will give you time to consider the reality of the offer—including the fact that you will be working at the company for (hopefully!) quite some time.

If the salary isn't what you had in mind...

Most often, college graduates entering the job market will be interviewing for positions with a narrow salary range—$16,000 to $18,000, $24,000 to $27,000, etc.—depending on the profession and industry.

If you are offered a salary close to the top of that range—$17,500 or $26,000 in the above examples—consider it a compliment and don't think too hard about pushing for more money. You don't have that much to gain anyway—particularly in today's performance-based job market.

But if you're offered a salary at the floor of the range, push for some more money. Tell the interviewer, "I understood that the position was paying as much as $24,000, and yet you're offering me only $21,500. You told me that you've interviewed several candidates for the position. Well, you've selected me because of my academic record and the drive I've demonstrated in securing top internships. Therefore, I believe a salary of at least $24,000 is reasonable for me to expect."

This will usually encourage the interviewer to come up in his offer a bit, though he might have been saving the top end for people with more advanced degrees or some experience in the field (despite what the ad said).

If you're still leaning toward the position, ask when you will receive your first salary review. If the answer is on your anniversary date, see if you can at least push for an earlier review to make up some of the shortfall between the offer and your expectations.

Tell the person making the offer, "I am very flattered by the offer and I wish we could agree on a higher salary. How about if you give me my first salary review in, say, six months, rather than 12?"

This is a rather easy concession for the interviewer to make. He will think that he is getting the candidate he wants for only half the difference between what you want to earn and what he wants to pay.

"How am I supposed to live on this?"

This might be a case of closing the barn door after the cow has escaped.

But if you are very surprised at the low salary offers you are getting during your first interviews, then you're, to quote former President George Bush, "in deep doo doo."

As you prepare to embark on a career, you should make sure that it is one that will fulfill your needs. And if a high salary is one of them, you'd better be aiming for a profession or technical discipline. If you expect to get $50,000 a year (or $30,000, for that matter) in your first job in, say, publishing, you're in for a rude awakening.

Before you go on your first interview, you should have gained, through your research, a pretty good idea of the numbers employers will be discussing with you when the question of salary comes up. If you're shocked the first time salary comes up during an interview, you are in for a bumpy ride on your way to your first job.

Look at the whole picture

I would encourage you also to look at the entire value of the compensation package. Some companies provide very generous benefits packages—including stock options, unlimited dental care, even company cars and free lunches along with "standard" health insurance and vacation days. If these benefits don't immediately add to your bottom line, at least you won't have to pay for them out of your own pocket.

Most company vacation policies are fairly standard: two weeks for the first three years, three weeks thereafter. Some companies offer "comp" time in exchange for a great deal of overtime. Some match employee deposits to retirement plans. Some require employees to contribute something toward health insurance. A number of benefits—such as profit sharing—may not be immediately available to you.

You should have learned something about the company's standard benefits package early in the game. If, at this stage, you find the offering abysmal, why are you still considering the job offer?

If there are any other questions you feel will affect your decision about whether to accept this job, you had better ask them now, while you are still considering the offer!

Remember, it ain't over 'til it's over

After all this work, I'm assuming you finally accepted an offer—somewhere! And that they're even going to pay you to show up. Breathe a sigh of relief and experience the thrill of victory in this tough job market.

However, this is hardly the time to relax and forget about all of the skills that helped you land this swell job.

Start off on the right foot by writing a letter to your new manager, telling him or her how much you're looking forward to "opening day" at your new company.

And don't forget to drop a line to your references and all of the other people in your network. Tell them where you've landed and how grateful you are to them for their contribution to the effort. These contacts will prove helpful to you—perhaps even on your new job. They are sure to grow more valuable over time, however, in the increasingly likely event that you end up in the market for a new position once again.

Once you start your new position, you'll be expected to live up to all of those wonderful things you said about yourself during the job interview. I'm sure that if you followed the suggestions in this book, particularly the advice on getting to know yourself, you'll do well in your first job—and during the entire course of your career.

Good luck!

Index

Your First Interview